Wagiaghaz'Ẹdo

(Wa gia gha z'Ẹdo)

A practical guide to learning the Ẹdo Language and its history

Osazuwa Ọmẹdẹ

Waghiaghaz'Ẹdo

(Wa gia gha z'Ẹdo)

A practical guide to learning the Ẹdo language and its history

'Urhu' Ẹdo Kevbẹ Emwin Arre'

Osazuwa Ọmẹdẹ

ISBN:

ACKNOWLEDGEMENT

Let me begin with a popular Ẹdo adage: 'Every mountain top is within reach if you just keep climbing.' I will, therefore, thank God Almighty who has given me the will to climb. I thank Him for the wisdom, inspiration, and guidance.

I also wish to relay my heartfelt gratitude to our king, His Royal Majesty Ọmọ N'Ọba N'Ẹdo, Uku Akpọlọkpọlọ. Ọba Ẹwuare II (The Great) for encouraging the teaching and speaking of our Ẹdo dialect as well as the preservation of our rich and inimitable cultural heritage.

Thanks to everyone, too, who has in one way or another, inspired, encouraged, and supported me in the arduous task of writing this book. My gratitude is boundless.

To my family, friends and every Ẹdo sons and daughters around the world.

Specially to my Children

Kevin

Sharon

Meredith

Dillon

Edrick

and my Queen Ivie (Chidimma).

INTRODUCTION

Amazẹ ẹvbu'ọmwan eta wii is a Benin or Ẹdo word that translates loosely as 'anyone who cannot relate effectively in his own dialect or his mother tongue, is lost.'

It is the above aphorism that really drove me into writing this handbook. A man's identity and his language are two mutually inclusive concepts. They are inseparable and bound together. Just as a Peruvian of the Andes is tied to his culture and able to relate convincingly in his local dialect of Quechua, so am I proud to relate in my beautiful dialect of Ẹdo. Who would not be proud of his or her ancestral heritage after all?

Wagiaghaz'Ẹdo, which you are about to read is a practical guide to learning the Ẹdo language. It is brief but will be extremely useful to all ages. It is simple to follow – and begins from the embryonic stage of learning the Ẹdo language: its alphabets, pronunciation, consonants, and known phrases.

Amongst the Ẹdos, I have also included the Esan (Ishan) tribe, who in reality, are our kith and kin as well as partners-in-progress in transforming Edo State into being a force to be reckoned with in the annals of Nigeria's history. In cognisance of their contribution, it should be recalled that they (the Esan tribe), produced the first executive governor of Ẹdo (then Bendel State), the late Professor Ambrose Alli of the blessed memory.

Wagiaghaz'Ẹdo also introduces readers to our songs, poems as well as the very tenets of our rich cultural as well as ancestral heritage. You will also get acquainted with a cream of Ẹdo musicians and other notable men and women of Ẹdo extraction.

Please enjoy!

Table of Contents

HIS ROYAL MAJESTY
OMO N'OBA N'EDO, UKU AKPOLOKPOLO
OBA EWUARE II
OBA OF BENIN

SECTION 1:

LEARNING TO SPEAK THE ẸDO LANGUAGE

WẸDO NA ZẸ

ALPHABETS - IKPẸMWẸN VBẸDO

BIG LETTERS/small LETTERS - ABIDI NOKHUA/abidi nekhere

Aa	Bb	Dd	Ee	Ẹẹ
Ff	Gg	Hh	Ii	Kk
Ll	Mm	Nn	O0	Ọọ
Pp	Rr	Ss	Tt	Uu
Vv	Ww	Yy	Zz	

ALPHABETS PRONUNCIATION GUIDE
VBE NAYA TIRAN ABIDI

Aa ... Are /At

Bb ... Be /Bee

Dd ... The /Dii

Ee ... A /Cake or Abel

Ẹẹ ... Err /Pet or Egg

Ff ... Fee /Feel

Gg ... Gill /Gift or Girl

Hh ... He /He

Ii ... E /eel

Kk ... k /Okay

Ll ... Lay /Lay

Mm ... Me /Mean

Nn ... Nil /Need

Oo ... oh /Owner or open

Ọọ ... or /Orange or onions

Pp ... P /Pea

Rr ... Rill /Ring

Ss ... See /Seed

Tt ... Tea /Tea

Uu ... Uh /Put

Vv ... V /Victoria

Ww ... We /Williams

Yy ... Yee /Yield or yet

Zz ... Zee /Zip

Note: The Alphabet E in Ẹdo language will sound like A in English

English Alphabets/ Abidi Vb' Ebo

Aa	Bb	Cc	Dd	Ee	Ff	Gg	Hh	Ii	Jj
Kk	Ll	Mm	Nn	Oo	Pp	Qq	Rr	Ss	Tt
Uu	Vv	Ww	Xx	Yy	Zz				

CONSONANTS AND VOWELS

There are 21 consonants in English alphabets, which are B, C, D, F, H, J, K, M, N, P, Q, R, S, T, V, W X, Y, Z. although, Y sometimes function as a vowel e.g. dry. However, Ẹdo alphabets contain 17 consonants which are B, D, F, H, K, L, M, N, P, R, S, T, V, W, Y, Z.

While the English vowels are A, E, I, O. U and sometimes y, Ẹdo vowels are somewhat different - some additions are made thus: A, E, Ẹ, I, O, Ọ and U.

VOWELS

Aa ... Anikhi - meaning (Who is it)

Ee ... Ebaba - meaning (Father)

Ẹẹ ... Ẹzẹ - meaning (River)

Ii ... Igho - meaning (Money)

Oo ... Oghọghọ - meaning (Happiness)

Ọọ ... Ọdọ - meaning (Husband)

Uu ... Udu - meaning (heart)

Some examples of names with vowel alphabet

Aa ... Adesuwa and Adọlọr

Ee ... Ediọnwẹ and Emotan

Ẹẹ ... Ẹfosa and Ẹwuare

Oo ... Osazuwa and Osagie

Ọọ ... Ọmẹdẹ and Ọmobude

Uu ... Ugiagbe and Uwaifo

DOUBLE CONSONANTS (AGBEVA)

Double consonants generally help to spell most words correctly in English alphabets. Examples are 'bar' (barred/barring) or 'rob' (robbed/robber). Same with Edo language; below are double consonants in Ẹdo alphabet.

GB ... A**gb**ọn - meaning (Life)

GH ... I**gh**o - meaning (Money or Cash)

KH ... O**kh**a - meaning (Story)

KP ... U**kp**ọn - meaning (Cloth)

MW ... E**mw**anta - meaning (Truth)

RH ... E**rh**an - meaning (Wood)

RR ... (La)**rr**e - meaning (to come)

VB ... U**vb**i - meaning (Princess)

Other examples of Ẹdo words with Double consonants with are E**gb**e/Body, Ẹ**gh**ẹ/Time, Ekhwe/Shame, U**kp**u/cup, E**mw**in/Thing or Matter, **Rh**ie/to take, (I)**rr**enẹ/I have arrived, **Rr**ie' vbare/to eat food, and Ẹ**vb**o/Town or City.

In Ẹdo language grammatology, there are other sets of double letters, the mastery of which will help in spelling some words correctly. Since the letters are used together to complete some certain pronunciation, they have been coined 'collocated letters'. The following are collocated letters in Ẹdo language: AN, ẸN, IN, ỌN, UN. Although each set is a combination of a vowel letter and a consonant letter, together they form a single consonant sound, and this seems to be pronounced through the nose (Ola na lẹ ihue ta).

OLA NA LẸ IHUE TA

AN ... Av**an** - meaning (Afternoon)

ẸN ... Eh**ẹn**-meaning (Fish)

IN ... Ih**in**rọn-meaning (Seven)

ỌN ... Ay**ọn** - meaning (Drink)

UN ... Uh**un** - meaning (Head)

Lady Erosion Lauretta

Musical Artist

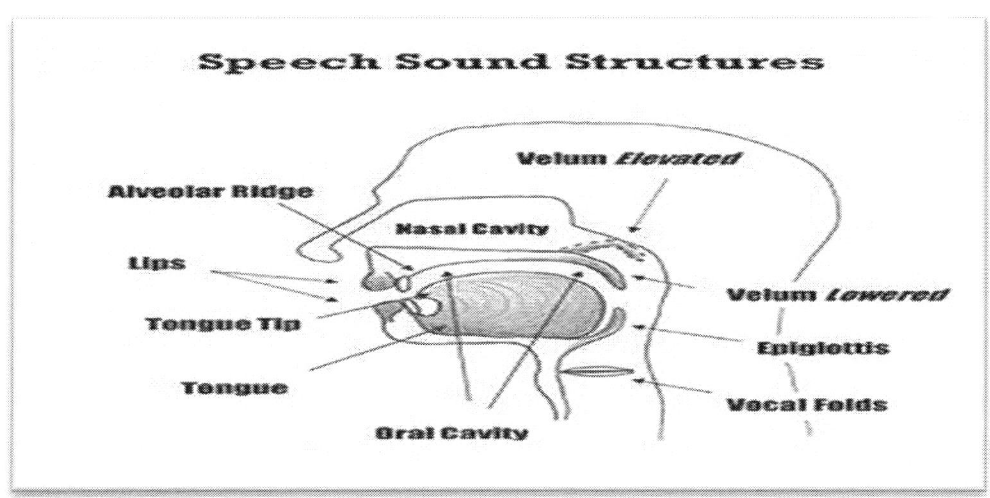

(Google Image, 2020)

INTRODUCING YOURSELF IN ẸDO LANGUAGE

- Who is at home? ... Arowa? **/**RESPONSE. Mẹ nẹ Amẹnaghawọn nọ - meaning (it is me Amẹnaghawọn)
- Hello! or, how are you? ... Vb'ọ ye rẹ? /RESPONSE. Ọ y' ẹse/ Ọ wa y' ese - meaning (I am fine/ I am doing great)
- Who is there? ... Arevba? /RESPONSE. Mẹnọn - meaning (it is me)
- Who is this? ... Anakhin? /RESPONSE. Mẹnọn - meaning (it is me)
- Who is it? ... Anọ? /RESPONSE. Mẹnọn - meaning (it is me)
- What? ... vbọkhin? /RESPONSE. Ẹre mwin rhọkpa - meaning (it is nothing)
- What? ... D'Emwin? /RESPONSE. Ọse mwẹn ẹ r'idomiẹn - meaning (I came to see my friend)
- What time is it? ... Inu ẹgogo ọhe tu? /RESPONSE. Ẹgo eva ọtu - meaning (its 2 o'clock)
- What is your friend's name? ... vb' ọrẹ Eni ọgh'ọserhuẹ? /RESPONSE. Imafidọn Omoregie a tiẹ ọse mwẹn - meaning (Imafidọn Omoregie is my friend's name
- Which among them? ... D' enọkhin vbọ? /RESPONSE. Enọ tan sẹ - meaning (the tallest)
- What is your name? ... Vb' a tie rhuẹ? /RESPONSE. Osazuwa a tie mwẹn - meaning (My name is Osazuwa)
- What is your father's name? ... Vb 'ọre Eni Era rhuẹ? /RESPONSE. Eni Era mwẹn ọ r' Ọmẹdẹ - meaning (My father's name is Ọmẹdẹ)
- What is your mother's name? ... Vb 'ọ re Eni' ye rhuẹ? /RESPONSE. Eni' ye mwẹn ọ r' Dora - meaning (My mother's name is Dora)
- How old are you? ... In' Ukpo ọ r' u ye? /RESPONSE. Ukpo Enẹyan-iyeva ẹ r' I ye - meaning (I am 44 years old)
- Where do you come from? ... D' Eke n' u ke rre? /RESPONSE. Uselu ẹ r' I ke rre - meaning (I am from Uselu)

MEETING SOMEONE FOR THE FIRST TIME

- Koyo ọse mwẹn, Vb'ọ ye rẹ? / Hello, my friend, how are you?
- Eni mwẹn ọ r' Osazuwa Ọmẹdẹ, Ovbiẹ Uselu ẹ r' ikhin, Elondon ẹ r' I ye. / My name is Osazuwa Ọmẹdẹ, from Uselu and I live in London
- ENollywood ẹ r' I na wina vbẹ UK, D' eke n' u ke dee? /I work with Uk Nollywood, where are you coming from?
- Vb, a tie wẹ? Ghi ma ghaẹ ọse / What is your name? let us be friends
- Emwẹn wẹ y' mwẹn / I like you

When you meet someone for the first time, the natural thing you do is to introduce yourself:

GREETING (OTUE)

Greeting in Ẹdo language is known as Otuẹ and it is taken seriously by the indigenous people. It is necessary for people to wish each other well through greeting. It is also believed that greeting defines one's character and when abandoned or deliberately ignored, one's dignity can be lost. Naturally, the young are expected to greet the elders. However, in some reversed cases the elders can also greet a young one who is unwell or sick: a classic demonstration that 'respect is reciprocal.'

Every family (Ẹgbẹ) in Ẹdo Kingdom has adapted one or more distinct methods of greeting according to or relating to their various historical backgrounds. In the ancient Benin Kingdom, the most significant greeting is Lamogun, which is solely for the Royal Family/Ọba family (Ẹgbẹ Ọba).

Note: When a woman is married into a family, she is expected to change her surname to the husband's family name. Furthermore, she must adapt to her new family's (husband's) greeting (Ukhu ẹgbẹ).

SOME FAMILY GREETINGS IN ẸDO (UKHU NA TUẸ VB' ẸDO)

- Delaiso (Laiso) - (First royal period from Ogiso era)
- Lamogun (Second Royal Period from Eweka 1)
- Lavbieze (Iyase of Benin)
- Laogele (Oliha of Benin)
- Latose (Edohen of Benin)
- Latose (Isiemwenro)
- Lagiesan (Ezomo of Benin)
- Lamosun (Ero of Benin)
- Laire (Eholor Nire of Benin)
- Laeru (Ise of Utekon)
- Layede (Iyase of Uselu/Ọmẹdẹ)
- Delauhe (Lauhe) - (Elawure of Usẹn)
- Layeru (Ezima (or Ojima) of Okeluhen)
- Lauvbe (Enogie of Uvbe)
- Dalaeho (or Laeho) - (Enogie of Ehor)
- Delaihon (or Laihon) - (Eholor of Igieduma)
- Delagun (or Lagun) - (Olokhunmwun)
- Lamodu (Umodu)
- Lamezi (Emezi)
- Lamore (Eni of Uzae (Ijare)
- Laide (Aide)
- Lamoru (Olumoru)
- Laloke (Oloke)
- Lamehi (Oloton of Benin)
- Laughe (Ughe)
- Laigie (Igie)
- Laugha (Ugha)
- Delaihe (or Laihe) - (Ohenukoni of Eviekoi)
- Delalu (or Lalu) - (Enogie of Irhue)
- Lavbiuwa (Enogie of Evbokabua)
- Lameri (Emeri)
- Lagia (Agia)
- Lamero (Eze)
- Lamehe (Emehe)
- Delakpan (or Lakpan) - (Akpan)
- Lamolu (Umolu)
- Laize (Ize)
- lamokun (Umokun)
- Lareni (Ureni)
- Laidu (Idu)
- Lairen (Iren)
- Laigena (Igiena)
- Lamekon (Emekon)
- Lagierua (Enogie of Erua)
- Lagba (Elema of Benin)
- Laire (Ogiamen of Benin)
- Larendo (Laidu) - (Ogiefa of Benin)
- Delani (or Lani) - (Ine N'Igun of Benin)
- Delaiki (or Laiki) - (Osa of Benin)
- Labo (Osuan of Benin)

- Labo (Enogie of Ugo N' Iyekorhionmwo)
- Labo (Osenugba)
- Labo (Ọdiọnwere N'Idumwun Ẹdo)
- Lagiewan (Iyasẹ of Udo)
- Delakun (or Lakun) - (Enogie of Ugo N'eki)
- Lagite (Enogie of ute)

Osawaru's family (Lavbieze)

Ivbie eze nọ zuwa

Ojo's family

(Lavbiekẹn)

Sorae's Family (Lamogun)

Asẹmota's Family (Lagipe)

COMMON GREETINGS

Greeting	Otue
How are you	Vbọ ye rẹ
Good morning	Ọb 'owię
Good morning (plural)	Wabowię
Good afternoon	Ọb 'avan
Good afternoon (plural)	Wabavan
Good evening	Ọb' ota
Good evening (plural)	Wabota
Hello	Koyọ
Hello (plural)	Wakoyọ
Hello	Doo
Hello (plural)	Wadoo
When you arrive home	Ọbowa
See you soon/later or Goodbye	Ọkhie vba zękpę
See you tomorrow/ till tomorrow	Ọkhian akhuę
Sate trip/ journey	Iyare
Well done/when someone is busy	Ọb'evbaru
Well done at work	Ọb' Iwina
Good Night/Till morning	Ọkhie Owię
Please be careful	Laho gha fẹko
Safe trip/journey	Okhian ẹwerẹ
See you some other time	Ọkhiẹn ẹdẹha

Lady Ọmọ

Lady Ivie Odẹh

Florence Iyamu

Edo Actress

It has been a while/ "long time"	Ọte sẹ ẹdẹha
Happy New Year/complements	Isẹ lo ogbe
Prosperous New Year	Ogbe ma vbe diaru
Thankful/Grateful	Kada (for male only)
No evil shall befall you (after meal)	Ẹrrhẹ ẹghigbuẹ (for female only)
You are the light I use to see	Wẹ ọre urrukpa n'ih ya dẹghe
You are my sweetheart	Wẹ ọre orrienrrien orhionmwẹn
I love you	Ih rhuẹmwen rhuẹ
You mean a lot to me	Ih kakabọ rhuẹmwen rhuẹ
You are the flower of my heart	Wẹ ọre oboboro orhionmwẹn
You are my pride	Wẹ ọre uyi mwẹn
Thanks	Urhuẹse

Omede's family in Graz Austria

Lady Kimberly Lawani-Idah (UK)

SOME COMMON VERBS

To Call	/	Tie	To Run	/	Rhulẹ
To Come	/	Lare	To Say	/	Tai
To Count	/	ke mwin	To Shake	/	Sogho
To Give	/	Rie	To Shake	/	weghe
To Go	/	GhaKhian	To Show	/	Rrhie ma
To Fight	/	Igbinna	To Sit	/	Tota
To Have	/	Mwẹn	To Stand	/	Mudia
To Help	/	Iyobo	To Start	/	Suẹn
To Lick	/	Lalọ	To Take	/	Rhie
To Look	/	Ghe	To Talk	/	Guan
To Peel	/	Bolo	To Tell	/	Tamaa
To Peel	/	kpalọ	To Untangle	/	Fanọ
To Pluck	/	Kọlọ	To Want	/	Gualọ
To Pour	/	Tue	To Work	/	Wina

To Sit (Tota)

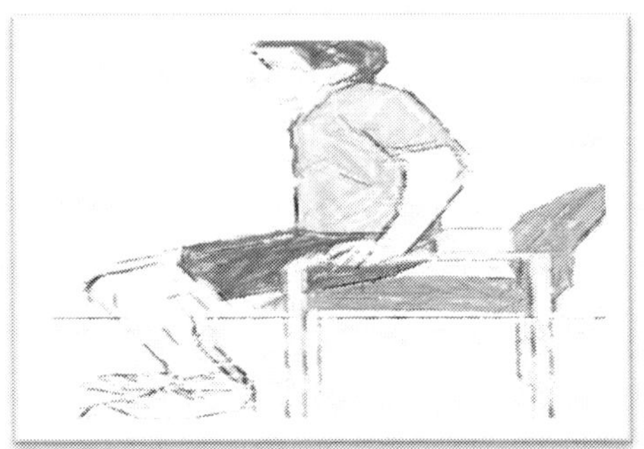

To Untangle (Fanọ)

SOME COMMON PHRASES

Stand by me /Mudia ke mwẹn

Stand up / Kpa egbe

Get up / Kpa egbe

Sit there/ Tota y' evbani

Stand here/ Mudia y' mwan

Come here / Lare mwan

Call me / Tie mwẹn

Come Out / Ladian

Come in / Lawa

Wait there / Mudia vbani

Look forward / Gho'daro

Look here / Ghe mwan

Look inside / Ghe uwẹrẹ

Look after / Gbaro ghe

Put it down / Mu yotọ

Tell me/ Tamaa mwẹn

Tell him/her / Tamaa rẹn

Take care / Gbaro ghe

Take away /Mugha Khian

Hold it / Daeyi

Give me / Rie mẹn

Give them / Rie n' iyan

Bring it / Muẹ rre

Come backward/ Lagho'di iyeke

Rita Omede

Mr & Mrs Osaruyi Airẹndẹ

SOME COMMON WORDS

Ok	/	Ọmaa	Pardon	/	Yabọ
Good	/	Ọmaa	My Lord	/	Noyaẹnmwẹn
Query	/	Guẹ gui			
Open	/	kie	You	/	Wẹ
Close	/	Gue	We	/	Ima
Cover	/	Ugue	Us	/	Ima
Fear	/	Ohan	Ours	/	Ima
Me	/	Mẹ	They	/	Ihian
			Them	/	Ihian
Theirs	/	Ihian	Kindness	/	Iruemwiẹnsẹ
Time	/	Ẹghẹ	Inseparable -	/	Naighisẹtinghae
Clock	/	Ẹgogo	Passion	/	Agiengien egbe
Quick	/	Zẹgiẹ	Troublesome	/	Ọruẹmwẹn
Unity	/	Akugbe	Affection	/	Igboriọn
Disgrace	/	Efa	Honest man -	/	Ọvb'ẹmwanta
Strength	/	Ẹtin	Humility	/	Imuegberiotọ
Power	/	Ẹtin	Sweet	/	Miẹn miẹn
God	/	Osa	Sweetness	/	Omiẹn miẹn
Almighty God	/	Osalobuwa	Humble	/	Ufumwẹn
Beauty	/	Imose	Humble person	/	Omwan n'ọfu
Spy	/	Yọnghe	Kindness	/	Ọmwizọhẹ
Prayer	/	Erhumwun	Brag	/	Oghagha
Heart	/	Ekhọẹ	Have arrived	/	Irenẹ

Which person / D'ọmwan

Which thing / D'emwin

How much / Inu

How many / Inu

Which place / D'eke

Which day / D'ẹdẹ

What kind / D'aro

What type / D'aro

What time / D'ẹghẹ

Meat / Emwiowo

Wealthy / Ọdafen

Cook / Ọlevbare

Author / Ọgbebe

Writer / Ọgbebe

Marriage / Orọnmwẹn

Naming Ceremony/ Izọmọn

Pause /Muen mudia

Marriage Ceremony/ Ugie Orọnmwẹn

Forgiveness / Ilekhue

Pardon me / Yabọ mwẹn

Forgive me/Ya lekhue mwẹn

Word / Ikpẹmwẹn

Sentence / Ifiẹmwẹn

Speech / Emwọnta

Statement / Itẹmwẹn

Go out / Ladian

Carry that / Muọni

Carry this / Muọna

Wish / Ahoo

Warning / Igbuhi

Keep silent / Gbẹdọr

Command / Evbawaru

Stammerer / Abẹmwẹn

One with a beard / Abetu

Approach / Abu

Caring for each other/ Adanegbe

Restaurant / Owua ogh'ulema

Mensuration / Mu'obomwẹn

Destroyer / Afian

Sword / Agbada

Ingrate / Agboghidi

Prostitute / Emamotu

Smallish person/ Ekekere

Stinginess /Emwindomwan

Question / Inọta

Mark / Ama

Exclamation / Esohie

Place on / Muyọ

Anger / Ohu

Remind me / Ye mwẹn re

Been a while /Ọkhiantesẹdẹha

Buy / Dẹ

Sell / khiẹn

Drink / Ayọn

Water / Amẹn

Sleep / Ovbe

Walk / Okhian

Body / Egbe

Hunger / Ohamwẹn

Shame / Ekhue

Long-life / Utọmwẹn

Better /Ọma'vberhiọ

Grace / Ẹsọhẹ

Forgive / Ilekhuẹ

Saved / imiẹfan

Fast / Awẹ

Fasting / Muawẹ

Food / Evbare

Book / Ebe

Dance / Gbe

House / Owa

Bath / khuẹ

Sleep / Ovbe

Market / Ẹki

Examination / Edamwẹn

Test / Edamwẹn

Good / Ọma

Not good / Ẹma

No / Ẹho

Yes / Ẹrhẹn

Right / Oberha

Left / Obiye

Walk / Okhian

Town / Ẹvbo

Life / Agbọn

Language / Ẹvbo

Progress / Alaghodaro

Blessing / Afiangbe

Lover / Egbakhian

Hurry / Zabọ

Heath / Egberanmwẹn

Cold / Oni

Stand / Mudia

Wait / Mudia

Patience / Iziegbe

Embrace	/ Dede	Businesswoman	/ Ọdụẹki
What	/ Vbọkhin	Trader	/ Ọdụẹki
What	/ D'mwin	Marketer	/ Ọdụẹki
Who	/ D'ọmwan	Wisdom	/ Ẹwaẹn
When	/ D'ẹghẹ	Good health	/Egberanmwẹn
Where	/ D'eke	Contentment	/ Ọyenmwẹn
Whose	/D'ọghọmwan	Calmness	/Ifumwẹngbe
Time	/ Ẹghẹ	Peace	/Ọfumwẹngbe
Road	/ Ode	Church	/Owugamwẹn
Here	/ Emwan	Hell	/Ẹrhinwin Erhẹn
Day	/ Ẹdẹ	Ship Captain	/ Oguokor
Star	/Orhọnmwẹn	Heaven	/Ẹrhinwin Ọfumwẹngbe
Moon	/ Uki	Spirit	/ Orhiọn
Wind	/ Ẹhoho	Preach	/ kporhu
Wealth	/ Ẹfe	Pastor	/ Ọkporhu
Street	/ Idumwu	Pastor	/ Ohẹn
Land	/ Otọ	Choose	/ Zẹẹ
Bush	/ Oha	Thing	/ Emwin
Press	/ Piẹn	Place	/ Eke
Write	/ Gbẹn	Satan	/ Esu
Learn	/ Huẹ	Junction	/ Ada
Farmer	/ Ọgbugbo	Crossroad	/ Ada
Hunter	/ Ohue	Area	/ Ẹdogbo
Businessman	/ Ọdụẹki	Farm	/ Ugbo

Slap	/ Ubi	Now	/ Ebaan
Musician	/ Ọkpemaba	Ugliness	/ Ikhọrhiọn
Student	/Ovbirhuemwi	Paid	/ Ọha osa nẹ
Driver	/ Ofimoto		
School	/ Owebe	Embrace	/ Dedemwen
Night	/ Asọn	Month	/ Uki
Night fall	/ Ẹdemu	Kiss	/ Munusunu
Day break	/ Ẹdẹgbe	This week	/ Uzọla na
Thunder	/ Avanukhun	Year	/ Ukpo
Harmattan	/ Okhuakhua	Lawyer	/ Ọmugui
Flood	/ Orhogho	Doctor	/ Ọbo
Week	/ Uzọla	Pastor	/ Ọkporu
My Darling	/ Naenmwẹn	Spokesman	/ Ọmunu
My Dearest one	/ Nonýaenmwen	Presenter	/ Ọkporu
Embrace	/ Dede	Police	/ Olakpa

- Primary school is called owebe nẹkhere, Secondary school is referred to as owebe nọkhua, while university is called owebe nọyosẹ.
- Church is also referred to as Ẹguosa (God's Palace). Holy-Aruosa Cathedral is an ancient church in Benin Kingdom where the Ọba of Benin fellowship or worship God and has a resident Priest (Ohẹn) that oversees the church activities.

FAMILY

Family / Ẹgbẹ
Relative / Ọtẹn/ Ẹgbẹ
Oldest relative / Ọkaẹgbẹ
My relative / Ọtẹnmwẹn
My relatives / Etẹnmwẹn
Parent / Nobiọmọ
Parents / Eni biọmọ
Child / Ọmọ
Children / Emọ
Man / Okpia
Men / Ikpia
Male adult / Okpiọba
Female adult / Okhuọba
Woman / Okhuo
Women / Ikhuo
Old man / Ediọnmwan
Old woman / Edede
Boy / Ọmokpia
Girl / Ọmokhuo
Yong man / Ẹghele
Youth / Igbama
Young lady /Ọvbonkhonkhuo
Young girl / Ovbialeke

Young girls / Ivbialeke
Baby / Ọmọmọ
Father / Erha
Father / Ebaba
My father / Erhamwẹn
Your father / Erhaa
Mother / Iye
my mother / Iyemwẹn
Your mother / Iyuẹ
Grandfather / Erhanọkhua
Grandfather / Ebaba nọkhua
Grandfather / Erherha
Grandmother / Iyenọkhua
Grandmother / Iyiye
Grandson / Eyẹ no okpia
Granddaughter/ Eyẹ no okhuo
Grandchild / Eyẹ
Great grandchild / Ihiẹnhiẹn
Great-great grandchild/ Ihienhien n'ogiọmọ
Great-great-great-grandchild/ Esakpaẹghodin

Great-great-great-great grandchild/ Ghabiọna

In-law / Orhuan

My in-law /Orhuan mwẹn

Mother in-law/ Iyọ'dọ

Father in-law /Erha ọghọdọ

Son in-law / Ọdafen ovbi mwẹn

Daughter in-law/ Ọvbokhon ovbimwẹn

My child / Ovbimwẹn

Children / Ibiẹka

Sister /Ọtẹnmwẹn nokhuo

Brother/ Ọtẹnmwẹn nokpia

Elder / Nọwanrhẹn

Elders / Eniwanrhẹn

Husband / Ọdọ

Wealthy man / Ọdafẹn

Wife / Amwẹn

My husband / Ọdọmwẹn

Your husband/ Ọdafọn

My wife /Ọvbokhanmwẹn

Your wife /Ọvbokhanrue

Friend / Ọse

My friend / Ọsevbẹn

Girlfriend / Ọse okhuo

Boyfriend / Ọse okpia

Partner / Ogieva

Enemy / Eghian

Bad friend / Ọsedan

Good friend / Ọse Ọghesi

School friend / Ọse ọgho'webe

Lot of friends / Ọse nibun

Festival / Ugie

Brother, sister (same father)/ Ovbierha

Brother, Sister (same mother)/ Ovbiye

Younger brother or sister/ Ọtẹnmwẹn nẹkhere

Older brother or sister / Ọtẹnmwẹn Nọkhua

Husband, Wife and Child

(Ọdọ, Amwẹn kevb'Ọmọ)

Husband and Wife

(Ọdọ vbẹ Amwẹn)

Ọba (King)

Grandmother (Iyenọkhua)

Baby (Ọmọmọ)

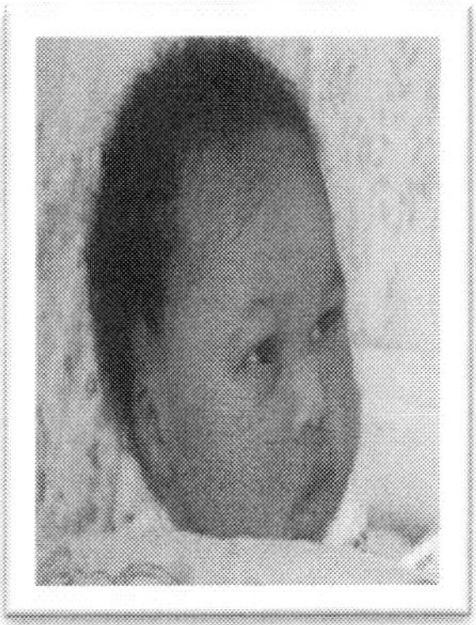

Father (Erha)

Baby (Ọmọmọ)

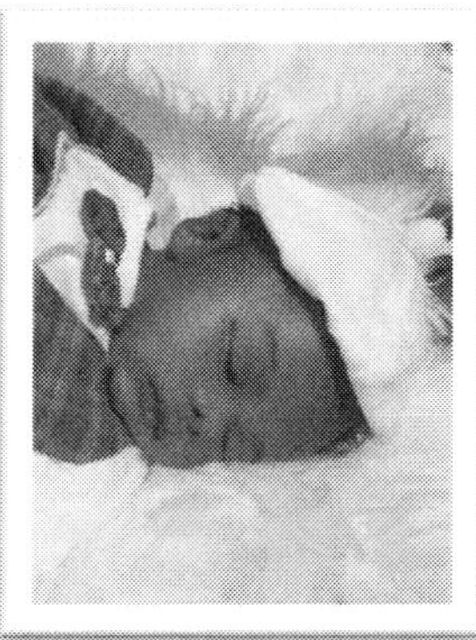

Mothers (Avb'Iye)

Ikpia (Men)

Chief Victor | Osazuwa | Owẹns | Chief Ogbẹmudia

Avbọ'se (Friends)

Influnce Akaba

Sylvester Umudi

Ikhayere Williams

Imafidon Ọ (Big Ben)

Mr & Mrs Ihama

Daiju Judd

Collins Ọbazgbọn

Juliis Ediọnwe

Ẹwaẹn Sọraẹ

Alex Ọbasẹki

Chief Ogiefo and friends

Uyi Ọdọbo

Ikhuo (Women)

PARTS OF THE BODY

ENI-EGBE

Hair / Eto

Head / Uhunmwun

Brain / Ẹrrerre

Lips / Akhuara unu

Eye / Aro

Eye lash / Ifuan aro

Eyeball / Ikpan aro

Teeth / Akọn

Nose / Ihue

Septal perforation/ Uvun Ihue

Nostrils / Uvun Ihue

Nasal hair / Eti' hue

Snot/Catarrh / Ihin

Tongue / Arramwẹn

Mouth / Unu

Ear / Ehọ

Armpit / Ihie

Underarm hair/ Eto ihie

Jaw / Agbanmwẹn

Throat / Ẹho

Face / Ugbaro

Neck / Ẹyaẹn

Shoulder / Izabọ

Right hand /Oberha ọmwan

Left hand / Obiyeọmwan

Chest / Ẹwẹ

Hand / Obọ

Fore hand / Ikpinhianbọ

Finger / Ihiẹn

Hand Finger Neil/ Ihien obọ

Palm / Atatabọ

Breast / Ewẹn

Back / Iyeke

Front / Odaro

Buttocks / Ikebe

Waist / Ẹkun

Hip / Ẹkun

Buttock / Ikebe

Stomach / Ẹko

Navel / Ukhọn

Heart / Ẹkokudu

Leg / Owẹ

Toes / ikpianwẹ

Leg finger Neil/		Ihien owẹ	Anus	/	On'isan
Foot	/	Owẹ	Blood	/	Esagiẹn
Knee	/	Igbọn	Tears	/	ame've
Bone	/	Ugboloko	Vain	/	Inian
Penis	/	Ekia	Body	/	Egbe
The tip of a Penis/		Ukpekia	Soul	/	Orhiọn
Virginal	/	Uhe	Intestine	/	Ibiẹ'ko
Urine	/	Ahiọr			
Poo	/	Isan			
Fart	/	Ehun			
Elbow	/	Ukoko'abọ			

Nose (Ihue)

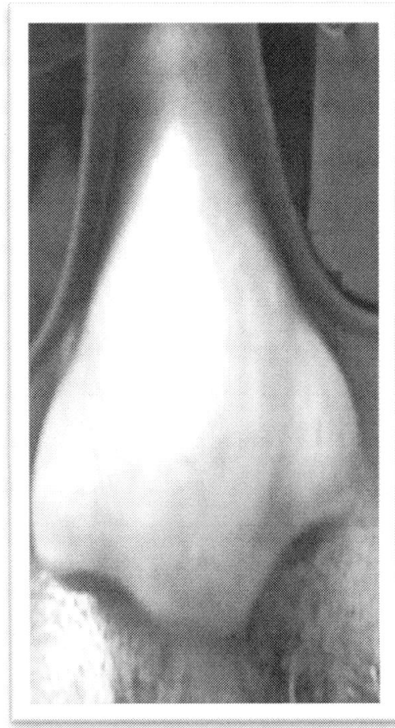

Ear (Ehọr)

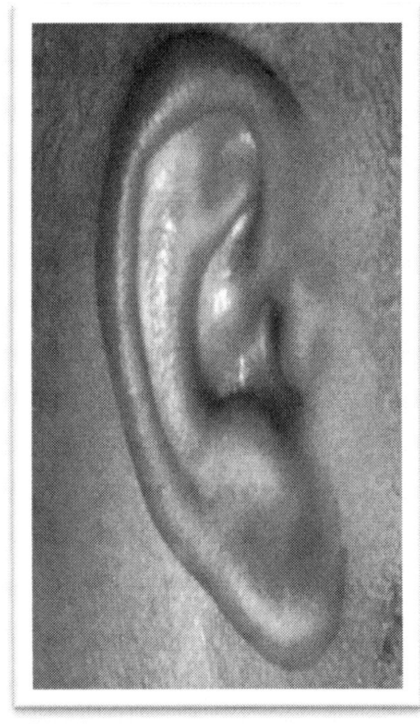

PARTS OF THE BODY (DIAGRAMS)

Eni-Egbe

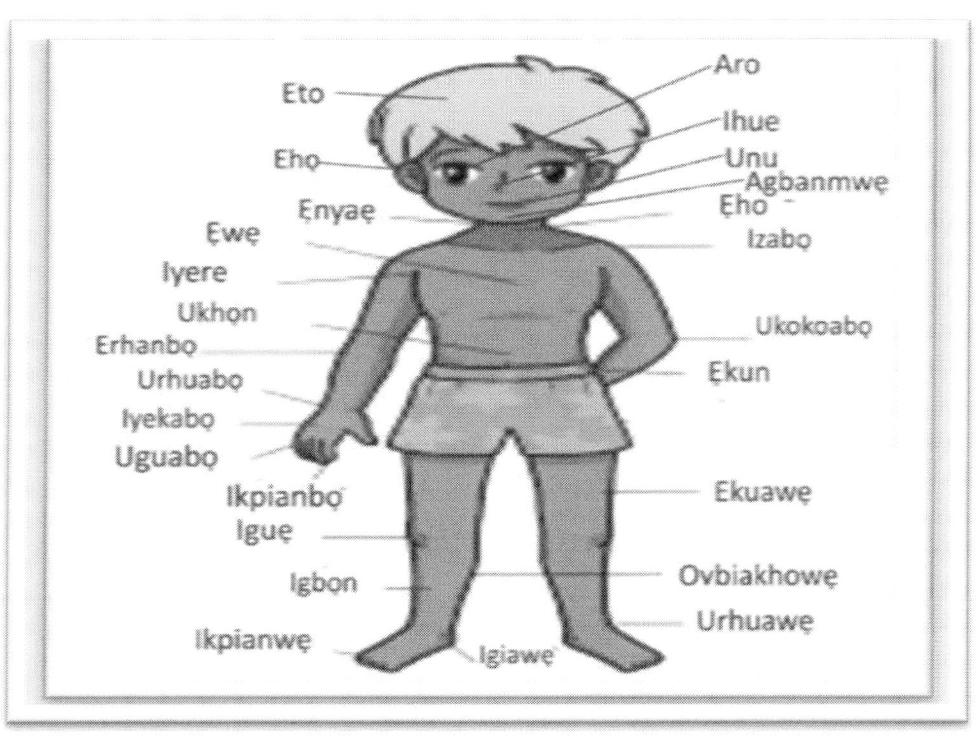

Eric Imadiyi and Favour Brown Imadiyi

CEO Exsto Euros Money Transfer (UK)

Juliet Erebọr Okonkwo

CEO, JULZ HAIR

PARTS OF THE BODY IN ESAN LANGUAGE

THE HUMAN BODY (EGBE ORIA)

Eye	/	Elolo	Arm	/	Uru-obor
Nose	/	Ihue	Elbow	/	Uguobor
Mouth	/	Unu	Waist	/	Akhiobor
Head	/	Uhuobhon	Fingers	/	Ikpian obor
Ear	/	Ehor	Fingernails	/	Ihien Obor
Round the ear	/	Egbehor	Between leg	/	Etagha
Eye lashes	/	Ighighin-elo	Hand	/	Obọ
Head hair	/	Eto-uhuobhon	Leg	/	Oranbhen
Shoulder	/	Hian-obor	Knee oranbhen	/	Uguele
Chest	/	Udu	Foot oranbhen	/	Atata
Neck	/	Uru	Toes oranbhen	/	Ikpian
Breast	/	Iyen			
Umbilical cord	/	Ukhon			
Stomach	/	Ekele			

Mouth (Unu)

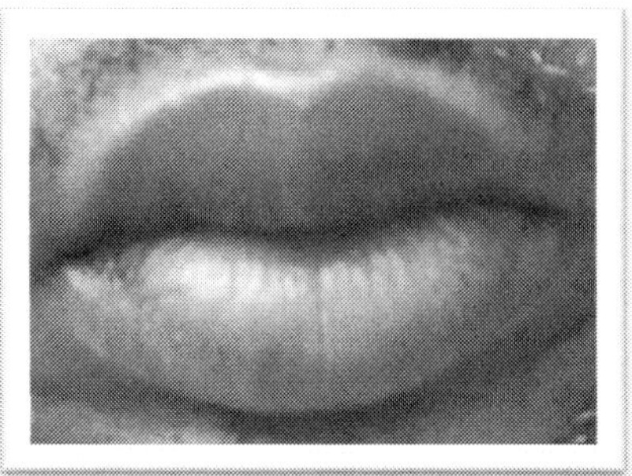

Eye (Elolo)

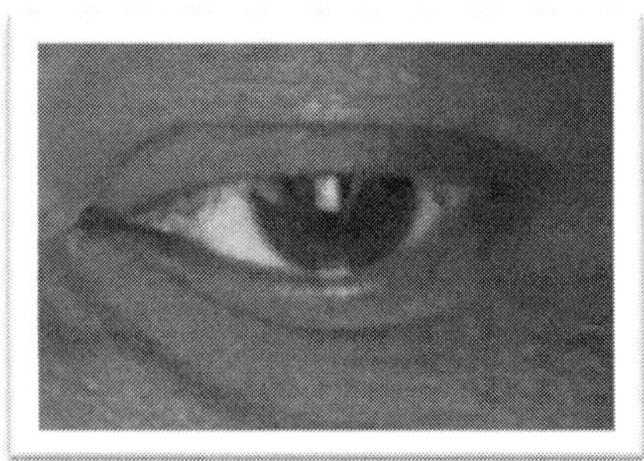

ANIMALS
ARHANMWẸN

Domestic animal/Arhanmwẹn owa
Wild animal /Arhanmwẹn oha
Reptile /Arhanmwẹn otọ
Antelope / Uzo
Alligator / Eghughu
Bird / Akhiamwẹn
Butterfly / ELabalaba
Black mamba / Ovbivbię
Brown rat / Ekuọmo
Bat / Ẹguẹn
Cattle egret / Elekeleke
Carnivores Animals/Arhanmwoha irriemiowo
Crocodile / Agbaka
Cockroach / Ehẹnmwẹn
Cobra / Obi
Chicken / Ọkhọkhọ
Cat / Ologbo
Cow / Emila
Cattle / Emalu
Camel / kętękętę
Chimpanzee / Ọsa

Dog / Ekita/Awa
Dove / Idu
Duke / Ekpękpęyę
Duck fowl / Izagua
Dragon fly / Obalamen
Elephant / Eni
Egg / Ekẹn
ỌKhọkhọ
Eagle / Akhua
Electric fish / Oriri
Earthworm / Ikolo
Fish / Ehẹn
Fly / Ikian
Frog / Ękiyęę
Firefly / Emunemune
Fox /Umuọkhọkhọ
Goat / Ewe
Glow worm /Emunemune
Grasscutter / Evuato
Hare / Orere
Horse / Ęsin
Hawk / Ahuara

Hyena	/	Akpakoniza	Rabbit	/	Ọfiotọ
Hippopotamus	/	Eniamen	Rattle snake	/	Aka
Lion	/	Oduma	Sparrow	/	Ahianmwosa
Lizard	/	Ozikpalọ	Shrimp	/	Enitan
Monkey	/	Emẹ	Sand fly	/	Eriaria
Mosquito	/	Imuẹn	Spider	/	Akpakpa
Nightingale	/	Esikpogho	Sloth	/	Akuagha
Ox	/	Ẹmila Ẹdo	Sun Snail	/	Egilẹ
Owl	/	Esughusughu	Snake	/	Eyiẹn
Parrot	/	Okhuẹ	Tiger	/	Atalakpa
Porcupine	/	Okhuaẹn	Tortoise	/	Egui
Python	/	Ikpin	Vulture	/	Ugu
Peacock	/	Ahianmwose	Worm	/	Ikolo
Pig	/	Elẹdẹ	Tsetse fly	/	Udian
Rat	/	Ofẹn	Tilapia	/	Eboga

Goat (Ewe)

Dog (Ekita/Awa)

FRUITS, VEGETABLES AND FOOD

Orange / Alimo

Wood / Erhan

Lime /Alimo Nekhere

Pear / Orhun

Avocado /Orhunmwun Ebo

Velvet tamarind/ Ọmọugẹn

Banana / Ọghẹdẹ

Star Apple / Otẹn

Pineapple / Ẹdinebo

Plantain / Ọghẹdẹ

Tomatoes / Ekweamẹn

Corn / Ọka

Coconut / Ivin

Sugar cain / Ukhuere

Flower / Obobo

Pepper / Ehiẹn

Beans / Ere

Salt /Umwẹn

Vegetable / Afọ

Fruit / Ọmọerhan

Okra / Ikhiavbọ

Palm / Udin

Yam / Iyan

Kolanut / Ẹvbẹ

Groundnut / Isaẹwẹ

Bitter kola / Ẹdun

Onions / Alubara

Rice / Izẹ

Garri / Igahi

Water / Amẹn

Garden egg / Ekhue

Crayfish / Izenọfua

Prawns / Enitan

Spice /Ẹmun evbare

Akara (Bean cake)/ Eka

Boiled yam / Iyan nale

Pounded yam / Ema

Soup / Uwọnmwẹn

Banga Soup / Uwọnmwẹn ọgho'figbọn

Pepper soup / Ẹkhiobo

Okro soup / Uwọnmwẹn ọghi'khiavbọ

Ogbono soup / Uwọnmwẹn ọgho'hẹ

Bitterleaf soup/ Uwọnmwẹn ọgho'hiwo

Ogi/Akamu / Ẹkọ

Egusi soup /Uwọnmwẹn ọgho'gi

palm oil / Ofigbọn

Vegetable oil / Ororo

smoked fish / Ehẹn nakarẹ

Stockfish / Ebazabaza

Grounded crayfish/ Izenọfua nalọ

Peeled yam /Iyan nakpalọ

Coconut Rice/ Izẹ ọgha'mivin

Groundnut soup/ Uwọnmwẹn ọghi'saẹwẹ

Orange (Alimo)

Yam (Iyan)

Egusi soup (Uwọnmwẹn ọgho'gi)

Okra (Ikhiavbọ)

HOUSEHOLD

EVBALO VBẸ OWA

House	/	Owa
Palace	/	Ẹguaẹ
Mud house	/	Owẹkẹn
Room	/	Uugha
Wall	/	Egbekẹn
Kitchen	/	Ukoni
Bed	/	Uukpo
Pillow	/	Ukohun
Chair	/	Aga
Table	/	Agbaa
Door	/	Ẹkhu
Door	/	Urhu
Window	/	Oyọnghe
Compound	/	Ibare
Backyard	/	Iyekowa
Air	/	Ẹhoho
Ground	/	Otọ
Sand	/	Ekẹn
Courtyard	/	Ẹghodo
Toilet	/	Egbowa
Light	/	Ukpa
Fire	/	Erhẹn
Lamp	/	Urukpi' hue
Darkness	/	Ebiebi
Comb	/	Oyiya
Mirror	/	Ughegbe
Earring	/	Evbin'ehọ
Necklace	/	Emiegbe
Plate	/	Ọkpan
Knife	/	Erọ
Broom	/	Owẹẹ
Bag	/	Ẹkpo
Cup	/	Ukpu
Kerosene	/	Amẹ orhukpa
Matches	/	Usanna
Mortar	/	Odo
Pestle	/	Ovbiodo
Sponge	/	Ihiọn
Bucket	/	Ikoroba
Clay pot	/	Uwawa
Key	/	Isahẹn
Fan	/	Ẹzuzu
Fan	/	Ẹzuzu Ebo

Spoon / Ekuyẹ		Cloth / Ukpọn	
Mat / Ewa		Scarf / Ukhiọnfọ	
Bottle / Ọgọ		Handkerchief / Ukhiọnfọ	
Cutlass / Ọpia		Shoe / Ibata	
Phone / Utamuta		Cap / Ẹrhu	
Phone / Ukọemwẹn		Iron / Ulọkpọn	
Phone / Ovbiehimwin Ebo		Fridge /Ofuemwinre	
Needle / Olodẹ		Computer/ Ẹkpẹtin iwiwizin	
Bead / Ivie		Bicycle / Ikẹkẹ	
Pen / Ukeke		Car / Okotọ	
Basket / Okhuaẹ		Boat / Okọ	
Tread / Orhu		Airplane / Okẹhoho	
Trouser / Italawẹ		Ship / Okẹzẹ	
Shirt / Ẹwu			

Mortar (Odo) and Pestle (Ovbiodo)

Car (Okotọ)

MONTHS AND DAYS OF THE WEEK

Months of the year (Month means Uki)

January	/	Uki-Aguẹ
February	/	Uki-Ifie
March	/	Uki-Egbọ
April	/	Uki-Ekhuen
May	/	Uki-Egua
June	/	Uki-Ikpẹsi
July	/	Uki-Iviema
August	/	Uki-Ohiẹ
September	/	Uki-Ehọ
October	/	Uki-Emorhọ
November (Ewe)	/	Uki-Ihayan
December	/	Uki-Iguẹ

Days of the week (Ẹduzọla)

Monday	/Uzọla Ẹdẹgbe
Tuesday	/Aduẹ Uzọla Ẹdẹha
Wednesday	/ Adesẹ Uzọla
Thursday	/Uzọla Ẹdẹe Enẹ
Friday	/Irakhuẹ Uzọla
Saturday	/ Uzọla Nekherha
Sunday	/ Uzọla Nokhua

FOUR CARDINAL POINTS

North	/	Okuọ
West	/	Orhiẹ
South	/	Eken
East	/	Ahọ

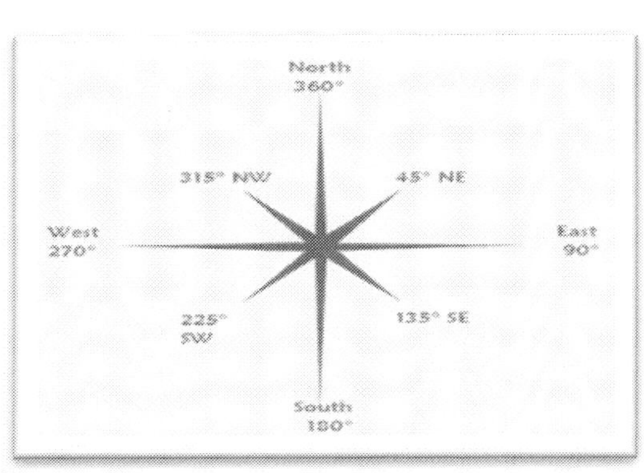

NUMBERS
IKEMWIN

Owo / One

Eva / Two

Eha / Three

Enẹn / Four

Isẹn / Five

Ehan / Six

Ihinrọn / Seven

Erẹnrẹn / Eight

Ihinrin / Nine

Igbe / Ten

Owọrọ / Eleven

Iweva / Twelve

Iweha / Thirteen

Iwenẹn / Fourteen

Ekesugie / Fifteen

Enẹn ẹi rrọ vbẹ ugie/ Sixteen

Eha ẹi rrọ vbẹ ugie/ Seventeen

Eva ẹi rrọ vbẹ ugie/ Eighteen

Okpa ẹi rrọ vbẹ ugie/ Nineteen

Ugie / Twenty

Okpa yaẹn ugie / Twenty-one

Eva yaẹn ugie / Twenty-two

Eha yaẹn ugie /Twenty-three

Enẹn yaẹn ugie /Twenty-four

Isẹn yaẹn ugie / Twenty-five

Enẹn ẹi rrọ vbẹ ọgban/ Twenty-six

Eha ẹi rrọ vbẹ ọgban/ Twenty-seven

Eva ẹi rrọ vbẹ ọgban/ Twenty-eight

Okpa ẹi rrọ vbẹ ọgban/ Twenty-nine

Ọgban / Thirty

Okpa yaẹn ọgban/ Thirty-one

Eva yaẹn ọgban / Thirty-two

Eha yaẹn ọgban/ Thirty-three

Enẹn yaẹn ọgban/ Thirty-four

Isẹn yaẹn ọgban/ Thirty-five

Enẹn ẹi rrọ vbẹ iyeva/ Thirty-six

Eha ẹi rrọ vbẹ iyeva/ Thirty-seven

Eva ẹi rrọ vbẹ iyeva/ Thirty-eight

Okpa ẹi rrọ vbẹ iyeva/ Thirty-nine

Iyeva / Fourty

Okpa yaẹn iyeva/ Fourty one

Eva yaẹn iyeva/ Fourty two

Eha yaẹn iyeva/ Fourty three

Enẹn yaẹn iyeva/ Fourty four

Isẹn yaẹn iyeva/ Fourty five

Enẹn ẹi rrọ vbẹ ekigbesiyeha/ Fourty six

Eha ẹi rrọ vbẹ ekigbesiyeha/ Fourty seven

Eva ẹi rrọ vbẹ ekigbesiyeha/ Fourty eight

Okpa ẹi rrọ vbẹ ekigbesiyeha/ Fourty nine

Ekigbesiyeha / Fifty

Okpa yaẹn ekigbesiyeha/ Fifty-one

Eva yaẹn ekigbesiyeha/ Fifty-two

Eha yaẹn ekigbesiyeha/ Fifty-three

Enẹn yaẹn ekigbesiyeha/ Fifty-four

Isẹn yaẹn ekigbesiyeha/ Fifty-five

Enẹn ẹi rrọ vbẹ iyeha /Fifty-six

Eha ẹi rrọ vbẹ iyeha /Fifty-seven

Eva ẹi rrọ vbẹ iyeha /Fifty-eight

Okpa ẹi rrọ vbẹ iyeha /Fifty-nine

Iyeha / Sixty

Okpa yaẹn iyeha/ Sixty-one

Eva yaẹn iyeha /Sixty-two

Eha yaẹn iyeha /Sixty-three

Enẹn yaẹn iyeha/ Sixty-four

Isẹn yaẹn iyeha/ Sixty-five

Enẹn ẹi rrọ vbẹ ekigbesiyenẹn/ Sixty-six

Eha ẹi rrọ vbẹ ekigbesiyenẹn/ Sixty-seven

Eva ẹi rrọ vbẹ ekigbesiyenẹn/ Sixty-eight

Okpa ẹi rrọ vbe ekigbesiyenẹn/ Sixty-nine

Ekigbesiyenẹn / Seventy

Okpa yaẹn ekigbesiyenẹn/ Seventy-one

Eva yaẹn ekigbesiyenẹn/ Seventy-two

Eha yaẹn ekigbesiyenẹn/ Seventy-three

Enẹn yaẹn ekigbesiyenẹn / Seventy-four

Isen yaẹn /Seventy-five

Enẹn ẹi rrọ vbẹ iyenẹn/Seventy-six

Eha ẹi rrọ vbẹ iyenẹn/Seventy-seven

Eva ẹi rrọ vbẹ iyenẹn/ Seventy-eight

Okpa ẹi rrọ vbẹ iyenẹn/ Seventy-nine

Iyenẹn / Eighty

Okpa yaẹn iyenẹn/ Eighty-one

Eva yaẹn iyenẹn/ Eighty-two

Eha yaẹn iyenẹn/ Eighty-three

Enẹn yaẹn iyenẹn/ Eighty-four

Isen yaẹn iyenẹn/ Eighty-five

Enẹn ẹi rrọ vbẹ ekigbesiyisẹn/ Eighty-six

Eha ẹi rrọ vbẹ ekigbesiyisẹn/ Eighty-seven

Eva ẹi rrọ vbẹ ekigbesiyisẹn/ Eighty-eight

Okpa ẹi rrọ vbẹ ekigbesiyisẹn/ Eighty-nine

Ekigbesiyisẹn / Ninety

Okpa yaẹn ekigbesiyisẹn/ Ninety-one

Eva yaẹn ekigbesiyisẹn/ Ninety-two

Eha yaẹn ekigbesiyisẹn/ Ninety-three

Enẹn yaẹn ekigbesiyisẹn/ Ninety-four

Isẹn yaẹn ekigbesiyisẹn/ Ninety-five

Enẹn ẹi rrọ vbe iyisẹn/ Ninety-six

Eha ẹi rrọ vbẹ iyisẹn/ Ninety-seven

Eva ẹi rrọ vbẹ iyisẹn/ Ninety-eight

Okpa ẹi rrọ vbẹ iyisẹn/ Ninety-nine

Iyisẹn / One hundred

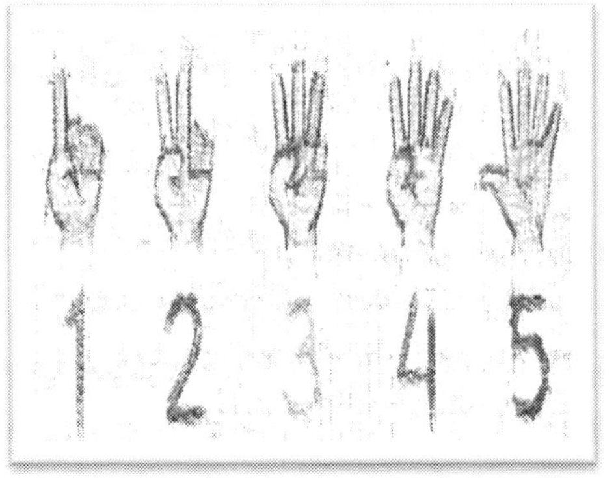

Mr &Mrs Dickson Osagie

SECTION 2:

HISTORY OF THE ẸDO PEOPLE

EMWIN ARRE Ọ̣GHẸ IVBI'ẸDO

A BRIEF HISTORY OF THE ẸDO PEOPLE

The word 'Benin' or 'Bini' originally called 'Ubinu' came into use around the year 1440 and 1485 respectively, during the reign of Ọba Ẹwuare, the Great. The reign of the 'Ogisos' (meaning 'rulers from the sky') was the first or earliest kingdom to oversee the affairs of Benin. This was between 900-1200 AD. The Bini kingdom demonstrates a striking similarity with the ancient Egyptian kingdom in terms of respect for constituted authorities and unalloyed devotion from the ruled.

The Benin Kingdom flourished during the Ogiso era, but the last Ogiso (Ogiso Owodo), proved unpopular amongst his subjects. He had one child despite having many wives. The dissatisfaction amongst his subjects resulted in his banishment. He later died, but his death was to bring about a leadership vacuum in the 'Igodomigodo' or Benin Kingdom.

After a long period of time, the people demanded for another king that would be of a blood lineage to the royal family, and this eventually led to the present usage of the 'Ọba,' with Ọba Ọrọnmiyan as the first king (about 1170 to 1200A.D). And Ọba Ẹwẹka I eventually became the second Ọba in 1200AD till 1235AD.

It should be recalled that Ọba Ẹwuare the Great was a vigorous, innovative, and popular Ọba in the history of Benin Kingdom. During his leadership, the Kingdom was completely transformed in all ramifications: religiously, politically, materially, and socially.

In the year 1897, the British Empire under the command of Harry Rawson, forcefully invaded the Great Benin Kingdom under the pretext of signing trade pacts. Their ulterior motives, however, was to overthrow our reigning king of that era: Ọba Ọvonramwen. The Ọba eventually surrendered after a fierce military battle which culminated in the brazen loot and unbridled thievery of our treasures and prized artefacts.

The king was exiled to Calabar with two of his wives. He died there in 1914. His first son who was also the crown prince had travelled to Calabar to retrieve his father's corpse, but was informed on arrival that his father, the king, had been buried three days earlier. He, the crown Prince Aiguọbasimwin was eventually crowned the 37th King of Benin as 'Ọba Ẹwẹka II.'

Currently, Ọba Ẹwuare II the Great (N' Ogidigan) is the Ọba of Benin. He was born in 1953, as Crown Prince Ehẹnẹdẹn Erediauwa. His Royal Majesty Ọmọ N'Ọba Ẹwuare II uniquely ascended the throne of his forefathers on his birthday, 20 October 2016, as the 40th Ọba of Great Benin.

The Ọba of Benin is the repository of our customary and tribal law. He is also the spiritual leader of the Ẹdo people, and is seen as one of the most appreciated, respected, and articulated traditional rulers in Africa.

The Benin people are strongly linked to other ethnic groups that speak the Ẹdoid or Ẹdo-like languages such as the Esan, the Afemai, the Isoko and the Urhobo. They live in small towns and villages and subsist mainly on farm produce such as plantain, cassava, corn, and other types of vegetables while livestock like sheep, goats, dogs, doves, crocodile, tortoise, duke, and fowl, are used for food and sacrificial offerings.

The Ẹdo people are rich in culture and tradition and are well recognised as the centre for arts and crafts in Nigeria. Their works in bronze, brass, carvings, and terra cotta are celebrated globally.

In a nutshell, when one thinks of Ẹdo (Benin) and her people, only one word stands out: Beauty!

Ọba Ovoranmwẹn

Ọba Erediauwa

The 18 Local Governments in Edo State

THE HEARTBEAT OF NIGERIA

1. Akoko-Edo (Central Akoko/North, Igarra/East Akoko, Ikpeshi-Egbegbere/Atje, Kakumo-Anyanran, North Akoko)
2. Egor (Agidigbi, Egor, Environ Camps, Evbougide, Iguediayi, Iguikpe, Oghedaivbiobaa, Oghokhugbo, Oviasuyi Camp and Ugbighoko)
3. Esan Central (Irrua, Ewu, Opoji, Ugbegun, Igueben, Ebelle and Ewossa)
4. Esan North-East (Uromi and Uzea)
5. Esan South-East (Ubiaja, Emu, Equare-Ewatto, Ewohimi, Ilushi, Inyenlen, Ohordua, Okhu-Essan, Onog-Holo and Oria)
6. Esan West (Eghoro, Ekpoma, Idoa, Naoka, Ogwa, Ujiogba, Ukhun and Urohi)
7. Etsako Central (of Ekperi, Fugar-Avianwu, Okpekpe and Okpella)
8. Etsako East (Agenebode, Agiere, Anumeji, Avhiodor, Bode-Waterside, Dapapa, Edegbe and Egori-Nauge)
9. Etsako West (Amahor, Ekpon and Ugun)
10. Igueben (Amahor, Ekpon and Ugun)
11. Ikpoba-Okha (Aduwawa, Agedo, Ekiuwa, Evbumufi, Evbuomodu, Ighekpe, Iguehana, Ogbeson, Ohovbe, Otenes Camp, Urora (UHOHO), Ute OKHA, Ologbo, Ajoki Akpes Camp and Avbiama)
12. Oredo (Gra, Etete, Ibiwe, Iwegie, Ugbague, Ihogbe, Isekhere, Oreoghene, Ibiwe, Ikpema, Eguadase, New Benin and Ogbe Ogbelaka
13. Orhionmwon (Aibiokunla, Igbanke, Oloten, Ugboko, Ugu and Urho-Nigbe)
14. Ovia North-East (Adolor, Iguoshodin, Isiuwa, Kokhuo, Oduna, Ofunm-Wengbe, Oghede, Okada, Oluku, Uhen, Uhiere and Utoka)
15. Ovia South-West (Iguoba-Zuwa, Ofunama, Ora, Siluko, Udo, Ugbogue, Umaza and Usen)
16. Owan East (Emai, Igue, Ihievbe, Ikao, Ivbi-Mion, Ive-Ada-Obi, Otuo and Uokha)
17. Owan West (Sabongida Ora- Iuleha, Ora and Ozalla)

18. Uhunmwonde (Egbede, Ehor, Igieduma, Isi North, Isi South, Uhi, Umagbae North and Umagbae South)

Mr Godwin Nọghẹghasẹ Ọbasẹki
Governor, Ẹdo State

RT. Comrade Philip Shaibu
Deputy Governor, Ẹdo State

PRAYER

ERHUN

IN ẸDO

Osa nẹ Erha mwan, Ivbuẹ ne giẹrẹ ima khin

Ma kevbe ibiẹka no re oto agbon hia, Su ima hia lẹ ẹdẹ nẹ rẹ fo

Ka aro ni ima, ki iyeke ni ima

Ghẹ gie imonto kuan ima, ghẹ ikẹkẹ kuan ima

Ghẹ gie ẹzẹ gbi ima, ghẹ gie uhae gbi ima

Ghẹ gie erhan bun rhu ima, mi ima fan vbe obo emwin dan hia

Rhie oyi hin ekhoe ima re, ghẹ gie emwan dan vbe koe yo

Rhie ohoghe hin ekhoe ima re, ghẹ gie emwan dan vbe koe yo

Rhie iyẹnho hin ekhoe ima re, ghẹ gie emwan dan bu ima ude dan

Sokpan, gie ẹwaẹn, kevbe iruemwiense

gha wan lele ima khan rhinrin

Isẹẹ.

IN ENGLISH

Our Father, we are your children

We and all other children in the world, See us all through today

Be at our front, be at our back

Let us not be hit by a car, let us not be hit by a bicycle

Do not allow the river to kill us, do not allow the well to kill us

Do not let the tree to break on us, deliver us from all evil

Remove stealing from our hearts, do not allow bad people to deceive us about it

Remove lying from our hearts, do not allow bad people to deceive us about it

Remove stubbornness from us, do not allow bad people to give us bad advice

But, Let wisdom, and a giving heart

Grow with us, forever and ever

Amen.

Mr & Mrs Isiwele

Dave (UK Artist)

Itohan Igbinidu (Actress)

Pastor & Pastor Mrs Igbinẹwẹka

Pastor & Pastor Mrs Osagbaekhọẹ

SOME ẸDO PROVERBS AND IDIOMS

ITẸN ẸDO ESO

- Aighi wu mu agbon rrie owa / One does not die and take his or her wealth a riches along. Life is vanity, so be kind while alive.
- Ẹdẹ uwu Ihoho fo / Everything ends with death, better to use your time positively while you can.
- Aighi yẹ ẹfe rriẹ umwẹn / Easy life is better and too much of anything is bad or have a negative side effect
- Ama zẹ ẹvbo ọmwan ah wiri / Importance of speaking one's language or dialect, every language is a system or symbols for encoding and decoding information
- Ama mu fua ah ighi mien rrie / importance of giving
- Aighi mien ọmwan n'ọfona / No one is perfect
- Eh vbe ah kor ah rrie ehe ẹre / What you sow is what you reap
- Ama rru khọ ah ighi wu khọ / one does not deserve to die for what he or she did not do
- Ama s'abe iwolo ai iwolo / Don't bite more than you can chew, and you cannot give what you do not have
- Arhuẹmwonmwan ọma sẹ aýon / Affection is better than drink consumption
- Ama talọ egbọmwan, aighi mie iyobọ / Ask and you shall receive
- Agbon n'ah vbare ah ýin / live your life the way you can
- Aighi rre ekpa, agha rre ubi / Be active or productive
- Agbon dinmwin / "Deep world" or the world can be uncertain.
- Unu agbon ighi t'ọkpa / when you cannot trust people's judgement. people will always have something to say about you good or bad but are not consistent.
- Ama khuan khẹ ota, ah ighi we ne ota mae ọmwan /He who do not plant should not wait for harvest. (No work no pay)

Itan Ẹdo man de fua

'The philosophy behind the proverbs of the great Benin people can never be obliterated, as the words of our fathers are words of wisdom. It is therefore, wise and beneficial to listen and adhere to the wise counsels of our elders'

Obọ naya gbọmọ ẹ r' aya si'ẹre k'egbe:

'It is the *same hand a parent uses to smack a child that is also used to draw him closer. In other words, parents should love and care for their children when they (the children) ask for forgiveness after committing an offence'*

Ọkpa gha viẹ ẹdẹ gbe

'Be patient in life'

Ẹki nado ẹse, ẹre erhe ye

'A well-managed business generates profit'

Idoboro ẹ r' ẹdẹ

'All is well'

Aiyi lvie rue emwin oya

'A prominent man never get involed in disrespect act'

Kizo Odaro - Edo Musical Artist

Urhu nọla

'Load voice'

Urhu nọla

'Outspoken'

Urhu nọla

'High-pitched voice'

Irriẹ egbowa

'I am off to ease myself'

Ima dọn ima fafara

'Still on course'

Juliet Esey Joseph

Nollywood/Italian Actress

Chief Lucky Nosakhare Igbinedion

Former Governor of Ẹdo State

Mr Lucky Ọmọsigho

CEO Ọbaland Magazine

Beckleys Ọkẹ (Edo Musical Artist)

Roseline Ogun

(Lizzy Kitchen UK)

Daniel F Osawaru

Founder UHDI (Uselu to the World)

POEM
(EKHARA)

Vbua rre? Aro

Fian mẹ, Ọfoo

vbọ'fo na?

Ọfo ni' te

Vbọ ẹ ite?

Ite aro

Vbọ ẹ aro?

Aro eba

Vbọ ẹ eba?

Eba Ẹlẹma

Vbọ Ẹlẹma?

Ẹlẹma Ighede

Vbọ ẹ Ighede?

Ighede Asabọ

Vbọ ẹ Asabọ?

Asabọ Ẹguaẹ

Vbọ ẹ Ẹguaẹ?

Ẹguaẹ Ọghẹnẹ

Vbọ ẹ Ọghẹnẹ?

Ọghẹnẹ Osa

Vbọ ẹ Osa?

Osa nọ biẹ imẹ gbọghọdọ, nọ biẹ uwẹ tẹkpu.

Sonia Aimy

Precious Osayandẹ

Richard Iyasẹrẹ (DaddyRich)

Businessman, Policia, Enetrtainer and Philantropist

Linda Joseph (Entrepreneur)

Beny Ellescious 24Bits

ẸDO SONGS

IHUẸN ẸDO

Uki (Moon)

Uki oh, Ba nẹ dẹ

Uki oh

Ba nẹ dẹ

D'vbi nigha rie nuki, nọ ba nẹ dẹ oh

Ba nẹ dẹ gbe

Oh, yemwẹn oh

Uki oh

Baa nẹ dẹ

Uki oh

Ba nẹ dẹ

D'vbi nigha rie nuki, nọ ba nẹ dẹ oh

Ba nẹ dẹ gbee

CHILDREN'S SONG

Yọ a ghe rhan, Yọ a ghi'rri

Yọ a ghe ke n'ebe nagben ebe

Urherhe oh Ẹwẹrẹ

Seventeen eighteen, Nineteen bọbọ

Seventeen eighteen

Nineteen bọbọ

Amb. JJ Barry
Founder and CEO
Edo Festival and Awards
(Promoting Edo Cultural Values Globally)

Osarobo Dickson Igbinosun
CEO 24BITS

Promoting Cultural heritage, Artistic Endowments and Creating Platform for Talented Musician, Winning Souls for Christ through music, Event Organiser

SOME WORDS ASSOCIATED WITH ẸDO CULTURE

Ada / Scimitar always carried before the Oba

Ọba / King

Agba /Rectangular stool

Amazẹ / Moulded clay figure of a human being

Ẹbẹn /Sword of authority usually carried before the Oba

Edaikẹn /Title of the heir apparent to Benin throne

Ediọn Ẹdo / Ancestors of the Edo people

Ẹdo Ọrisiagbọn/ Edo is the cradle of the world

Eghaẹvbo / Counsellor

Eghaẹvbo n' ore/ Town counsellor

Eguaẹ / Palace

Ekẹn /Work free day

Ẹkete / Throne

Ekhaẹmwẹn / Chiefs

Enikaro / Originators

Enogie / Duke

Eruẹriẹ /Palace Harem

Ewaisẹ /Guild of physicians

Ibiwe / The youngest of the three palace societies.

Ibiwe n'ekhua/ Group of title holders

Igiohen / Chief priest

Igun / Smith

Igun-Ematọn/ Iron Smith (Iron caster)

Igun-Erọnmwọn/ Brass Smith (Brass/Bronze caster)

Ihogbe / A guild in charge of recording Oba's ancestors.

Iloi /Oba's wife or queen

Iwẹbo /The most senior palace society

Iwẹguaẹ / Palace society next to Iwebo in hierarchy.

Iyo'ba /Oba's mother (Queen mother)

Odibo / A steadfast and vigilant servant or messenger.

Ọdiọnwere/ Village head

Ogiso / Title of early Benin Kings, who were regarded as Sky Kings.

Ọba / The King of Benin

Ohen /Priest

Olokun /God of the sea

Olotu / Leader

Ọmuada /Sword bearer

Ugie / Festival

Uselu /The dukedom of the heir apparent to the Benin Throne.

Uzama /Group of Chiefs who officiate at coronation of Oba of Benin (King makers)

Uzama n'ibie / Younger Uzama who normally officiate as deputy

Chief Osarọ Eghe Idah (The Ọbazelu of Benin Kingdom)

Special Adviser to Edo State Governor on Political and Community Matters

Chief (DR) John Osamẹde Adun (JP)

(Aiyọbahan of Benin Kingdom)

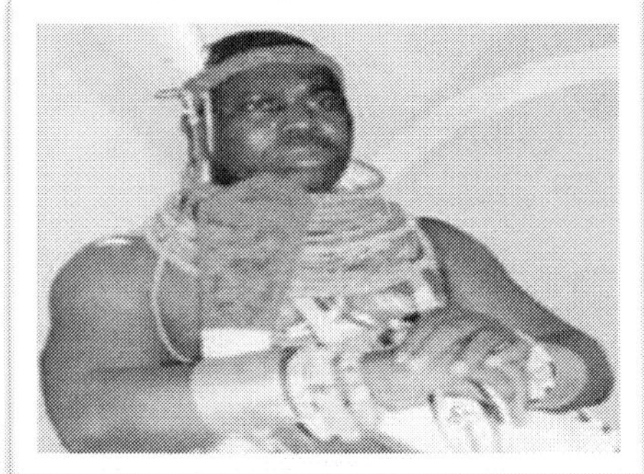

SOME ẸDO NAMES

ENI ẸDO ESO

Adọlọr
Aisọsa
Agbọnkọnkọn
Agbọntaẹn
Agbọnwanegbe
Aibuẹdẹfe
Aigbogun
Aihuọbabẹkun
Akẹngbẹdo
Akẹngboi
Akẹngbuda
Akẹnkpaye
Akẹnzae
Akẹnzua
Akugbe
Amẹghasihion
Abiuwairo
Adọkpagbeyuhun
Adọmwandagbọn
Ẹdunekhui
Ẹduwuirofo
Ẹduzola

Ẹfevbeokieke
Egbenayaloben
Egbeokaruwa
Egboghakan
Ẹguaemwense
Ẹguagie
Ehẹnẹdẹn
Ehengbuda
Ehiọzee
Ekenesenahenrien
Ekenọmaghele
Ekhenayahiore
Ekhorgiawe
Ekhorsuehi
Ekhorutomwen
Ẹkomwenrenren
Ẹkorowiro
Ẹkpenede
Emwiogbon
Enakhere
Enaruna
Enoghayiangbon

Enomaren
Enosagie
Erediauwa
Erokpaedamwen
Ẹrọnmwọn
Ẹseimuede
Ẹsigie
Evbaguehita
Evbakhamenhi
Evbakhavbokun
Evbakowierhu
Evbaruovbokhanre
Evbu
Evbuọmwan
Ẹwẹdọ
Ẹweka
Ẹwuakpe
Ẹwuare
Ẹzegbebe
Giegbefumwẹn
Ibierutomwen
Iduoriyekemwen

Ighiwiyisi
Ighodaro
Iguehide
Iguehimwenduwa
Ihanmwinran
Imagbe'nikaro
Imarhiagbe
Imasiokuebo
Itohan
Iyayomwaegbe
Iyengumwena
Iyenguwena
Iyonawan
Izehiese
Ọbanosa
Ọdoruyi
Ogbebo
Ogbeide
Ogbeiwi
Oghọghọ
Ọghomwọnyemwẹn
Oguola
Ogieva
ohuan

Okuomose
Olua
Ọmorogbe
Ọmọsọukpọn
Ọmozuhiomwan
Ọnaghise
Ọreoghene
Ọrobehi
Osaigbovo
Osaikhukhuomwan
Osariemẹn
Osasenaro
Osabuohien
Osarenkhọẹ
Ọsemwende
Ọvonramwẹn
Ọzolua
Uhunamure
Usevbinhiakhin
Uwaifiokun
Uwuakhuahen
Uwuigiaren
Aimiuwu
Akendayi

Akioyamen
Amayo
Edionwe
Ẹhimwẹnma
Enosakhare
Enosayaba
Idahosa
Idemudia
Idubor
Idusaye
Igbinedion
Igbinidu
Igbinọba
Igbinokun
Igbinosa
Igbinosun
Igiehon
Imafidọn
Imafu
Imaruaghẹru
Iyarẹ
Iyayi
Iyọha
Izẹvbigie

Nenhizẹna
Nọmayo
Nosakahre
Nowamagbe
Ọbagie
Ọbahiagbọn
Ọbapkọlọr
Ọbasẹki
Ọbasohan
Ọbasuyi
Ọbayantọr
Ọbazuaye
Ọbọmasọmwanikhi
n
Ọdigię
Ọdiọn
Ọdiọnwere
Ogbeide
Ọgbọmwan
Ogedegbe
Ogiemwọnyi
Ogieva
Ogunsuyi
Ohanenzę
Okosun

Ọlaye
Olotu
Ọmẹdẹ
Ọmọigui
Ọmọnfọmwan
Ọmọngiatẹ
Ọmọnkaro
Ọmọregie
Ọmọsẹfe
Ọmọnọýan
Ọmọnregie
Ọmọnruyi
Ọmọnuwa
Omonzusi
Ọmọrọdiọn
Ọmwenyeke
Ọnaiwu
Osagbemwọrrue
Osaghaẹ
Osagie
Osagiędẹ
Osahọn
Osakpamwan
Osarogiagbọn

Osasuyi
Osayamen
Osayi
Osayọmonre
Osayuwamen
Osayuwu
Osazẹ
Osawe
Osazuwa
Osunde
Otote
Ọvbokhan
Ọviasu
Ọviawe
Owẹn
Ukpọnmwan
Umogun
Usuanlẹlẹ
Utọmwẹn
Uwagboẹ
Uwaifo
Uwazere
Uyiękpẹn
Uyigue

Uyilawa

Uwanguẹ

Imasuẹn

Aibuẹdẹfe

Giegbefumwẹn

Imasiokuebọ

Imasiokuọbọ

Ọdọruyi

Enaruna

Ogbeiwi

Ọmọrogbẹ

Imarhiagbe

Okuomose

Ehiozee

Iyẹnguwẹna

Osarọmẹn

Enakhere

Egbenayalobẹn

Egbeokaruwa

Aigbogun

Iyọnawan

Iyayomwaegbe

Evbu

Ebiuwairo

Efevbeokieke

Usevbinhiakhin

Aghazeruovban

Evbakhamenhi

Evbiehiomwan'iwio vban

Osasenaro

Erokpaidamwen

Orobehi

Uhunamure

Ekhenayahiore

Vb' ọ re Eni wẹ?

Eni mwẹn ọ r' Eghosa Ọbazgbọn

Philanthropist and Businessman

The Ẹdo naming ceremony (Izọmọ) is an act of choosing a child's name, which is usually performed on the seventh day after the child's birth. The ceremony is not only colourful, buy symbolises wealth and a sign of lineage continuity amongst the Ẹdo people.

MORE ẸDO NAMES AND THEIR MEANING

Abiẹmwẹnse /I am well bred

Abiẹyuwa / Amidst wealth/ a child born in affluence

Abighosa / Multitude that behold God

Abusọmwan/ Group of multitudes

Adọlọ /Peace maker

Agbọnyẹmwẹn/I love my world

Agbónwarhiẹnrhiẹn/ Life is good

Agbọnkpọlọ / The world is great

Aghabiọmọ / When one has a child, the child looks after the parents in old age

Aduwa / The beginning of greatness

Agbọndinmwin/ Life is far deeper from life

Agbónghamamwan/ When life is sweet for someone

Agbọnghamamwẹn/ I will prosper in this world

Aiguọbasimwinotọ/ One does not dispute the ownership of land with the King

Aghaleladia / one's actions is conditioned by his peers

Akugberẹtin /Unity is strength

Aigbediọn: / One does not beat one's elders

Aizẹhinọmọ / A child's destiny is not chosen by the parents

Aibangbẹ / One cannot renounce his extended family

Abiẹyuwa / Born into prosperity

Adesuwa/ Born during wealth

Agbọnifo/ World without end

Erharuyi / A child's honour derives from the father

Ẹdosọmwan / The Ẹdo land is greater than the individual

Ẹdorisiagbọn / The Ẹdo land is the source of the world

Ẹdogiawerie: / One cannot subvert Ẹdo land

Erhabọ /It is the father that protects one

Erhabude: /The father gives advice

Ehiọsu / It is the guardian spirit that guides

Ehimwẹnma / My guardian spirit is good

Ẹdoghọghọ / Happy day

Gumwẹndia / Remain with me

Ọnaiwu /This one will not die

Sonarae / leave this one alone

Ifuẹko / The Heart is calmed

Ivie / Precious daughter

Igbinigie / I seek to be protected by fiefdom rulers

Igbinediọn /I seek to be protected by the elders

Igbinẹwẹka /I seek the protection of Oba Ẹweka

Igbinnẹwuare / I seek the protection of Ọba Ẹwuare

Iyorre / I had left and returned

Osagiọbarre / King is ordained by God

Ọmọsẹfe: / A child is more important than wealth

Ọmọsẹde / A child is greater than a crown

Osamudiamẹ / God stood by me

Hon. Patrick Ọbahiagbọn

Ẹgogo (Bell)

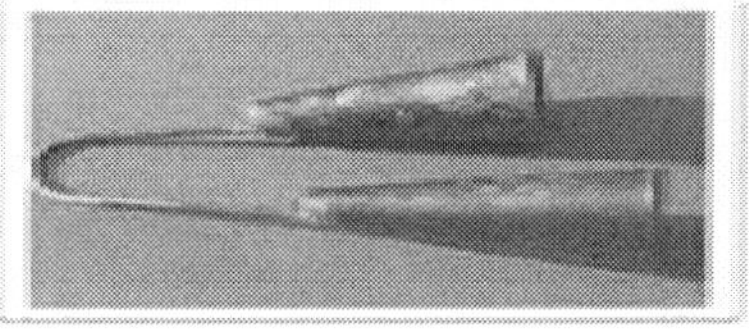

COMR. Lamptay IK Ọriakhi

Founder, The Comrade Show

SOME ESAN NAMES AND THEIR MEANING

Akhigbe	/	This one will not be killed
Aizehinomo	/	You do not choose a child's destiny
Akaehomhen	/	They are listening to me
Aigbojie	/	You do not fight a king
Asuelinmhen	/	Let my name be mentioned
Aiwanfo	/	One can never have infinite wisdom
Aiwansubhor	/	Death defies wisdom
Aiwanfoh	/	No one is completely wise
Abhulimhen	/	The verdict is in my favour
Enaholo	/	These are the ones desired
Ebemhen	/	What is good
Ejemhen	/	Good place
Edewede	/	The day still breaks
Ehizokhale	/	It is God who makes one great
Ekeleoseye	/	Beauty is in the heart
Eboseremhen	/	What God gave me
Ekan	/	Gold
Emoagbon	/	Issues of life
Ehiaghe	/	Looking up to destiny

Ty Precious Gold

Mr & Mrs Igiogbẹ

Mr Joe Ẹhi

Edo Cultural Ambassador UK

Ebimienbhagbon/ My life experience

Ivie / Precious child

Iluobe / I do no wrong/evil

Inegbenehi / I seek God's protection

Inegbedion / I seek the elders' protection

Ikuenobe / I will not succumb to evil

Inokpoare / I come from a great home

Iyebagbe / Not one to be killed

Ehimhen/Ehimen/ My guardian angel/Goodluck

Isokun / I have gotten to the top

Isowa / I have reached my house

Odalomeiye / I am at the forefront

Omoaghe / Because of the child

Oze / Silver

Oaikhena / I am wary of my family/home

Okosun / Son of shrine

Oseidobor / God does not make mistakes

Omonkhose / Child is the beauty of life

Omejele / Child of esteem, exalted one

Onakhuerekhanlen/ The pursued

Oseghale / God plans

Francess O. Okungbọwa

Nollywood/Edo Actress

Chief Owen Ọbasẹki

Mrs Gladys A. A

Educationist (UK)

Oshioikhina / I am wary of friends

Odianosen / It is well, fine

Omonzehio / Child brings pride

Okouromi / Son, friend of Uromi

Okoyomon / Son, friend of Oyomon

Okoinemen / Son, friend of Inemen

Okoemu / Son, friend of Emu

Idenekpoma / I am coming for Ekpoma

Ohainlo / Miracle, marvel

Okalo / First

Omonkhose / Child is the beauty of life

Otibhor/Otimhenbhor/ This makes me glad

Uwayemen / I love wealth

Roland Okungbọwa

Ovbi' Ẹdo Kpataki

Don Nice (Comedian)

Sunny Okosun

Traditional dancers

TWO BENIN DYNASTIES (OGISO AND ẸWẸKA-ỌBA)

LIST OF OGISOS (About 40BC -1100AD)

1. Ogiso Igodo (About 40.B.C - 16 A.D)
2. Ogiso Ere (About 16-66 A.D)
3. Ogiso Orire (About 66 A.D-100A.D)
4. Ogiso Odia (About 385 A.D -400 A.D)
5. Ogiso Ighido (About A.D 400-414 A.D)
6. Ogiso Evbuobo (About 414 A.D-432 A.D)
7. Ogiso Ogbẹide (About 432 A.D-447 A.D)
8. Ogiso Emehe (About 447 A.D-466 A.D)
9. Ogiso Ekpiegho (About 466 A.D-482 A.D)
10. Ogiso Akhuankhuan (482 A.D - 494 A.D)
11. Ogiso Efeseke (About 494 A.D. 508 A.D)
12. Ogiso Irudia (About 508 AD. - 522 A.D.)
13. Ogiso Orria (About 522 A.D-537 A.D)
14. Ogiso Imarhan (About 537 A.D-548 A.D)
15. Ogiso Etebowe (About 548 A.D-567 A.D)
16. Ogiso Ọdiọn (ABOUT 567 A.D-584 A.D)
17. Ogiso Emose (About 584 A.D-600 A.D)
18. Ogiso Oriri (About 600 A.D-618 A.D)
19. OGISO Erebo (About 618 A.D-632 A.D)
20. Ogiso Ogbọmọ (About 632 A.D-647 A.D)
21. Ogiso Agbozeke (About 647 A.D-665 A.D)
22. Ogiso Ediae (About 665 A.D-685 A.D)
23. Ogiso Orriagba (About 685 A.D. - 712 A.D)
24. Ogiso Ọdọligie (About 712 A.D. - 768 A.D)
25. Ogiso Uwa (About 767A.D-821 A.D)
26. Ogiso Ehẹnẹdẹn (About 821A.D-871 A.D)
27. Ogiso Ohuẹdẹ (About 871A.D - 917 A.D)
28. Ogiso Oduwa (about 917 A.D – 967 A.D
29. Ogiso Obioye (About 917 A.D- 1012 A. D)
30. Ogiso Arogho (About 1012-1059 A.D)
31. Ogiso Owodo (About 1059 - 1100 A.D)

LIST OF ỌBAS

1. Ọba Ọrọnmiyan (About 1170 A.D-1200A.D)
2. Ọba Ẹwẹka I (About 1200AD-1235AD)
3. Ọba Uwakhuanhẹn (About 1235AD-1243AD)
4. Ọba Ehenmihẹn (About 1243AD-1255A)
5. Ọba Ẹwẹdẹ (About 1255AD-1280AD)
6. Ọba Oguola (About 1280AD-1295AD}
7. Ọba Edoni (About1295AD-1299AD)
8. Ọba Udagbedo (About1299AD-1334AD}
9. Ọba Ohen (About1334AD-1370AD)
10. Ọba Ogbeka (About 1370AD- 1400AD)
11. Ọba Orobiru (About 1400AD- 1430AD)
12. Ọba Uwaifiokun (About1430AD-1440AD)
13. Ọba Ẹwuare the Great (1440AD-1473AD)
14. Ọba Ezoti (About 1473AD1473AD)
15. Ọba Olua (About 1473AD-1480AD)
16. Ọba Ọzọlua (About1481AD-1504AD)
17. Ọba Ẹsigie (About1504-1550AD)
18. Ọba Orhogbua (ABout1550AD-1578AD)
19. Ọba Ehẹngbuda (About 1578AD-1606AD)
20. Ọba Ohuan (About1606AD-1641AD)
21. Ọba Ahenzae (About1641AD-1661AD)
22. Ọba Akenzae (About 1661AD-1669AD)
23. Ọba Akengboi (About 1669AD-1675AD)
24. Ọba Akenkpaye (Abou1675AD-1684AD)
25. Ọba Akengbodo (About 1684AD-1689A)
26. Ọba Oroghene (About1689AD-1700AD)
27. Ọba Ewuakpẹ (About1700AD-1712AD)
28. Ọba Ozuere (About1712AD-1713AD)
29. Ọba Akẹnzua I (About 1713AD- 1735AD)
30. Ọba Eresoyen (About 1735 AD-1750AD)
31. Ọba Akẹngbuda (About1750AD-1804AD)
32. Ọba Ọbanosa (About 1804AD-1816AD)
33. Ọba Ogbẹbọ (About 1816AD-1816AD)
34. Ọba Ọsẹmwẹndẹ (About 1816AD-1848)

35. Ọba Adolor (About 1848AD-1888AD)
36. Ọba Ovoranmwẹn (1888AD-1914AD)
37. Ọba Ẹwẹka II (1914AD-1932AD)
38. Ọba Akẹnzua II (1932AD-1978AD)
39. Ọba Erediauwa (1978AD-2016 AD)
40. Ọba Ẹwuare II the Great (2016AD-Date)

His Royal Majesty Ọmọ N'Ọba N'Ẹdo

Uku Akpọlọkpọlọ Ẹwuare II (The Great)

Ọba of Benin Kingdom

SOME BENIN ENOGIES AND CHIEFS

ENOGIES (DUKES)

- H.R.H, N. Ohenzuwa (Enogie of Evbomodu)
- H.R.H, O.O. Osemwende (Enogie of Uteh N' Urekpoki)
- H.R.H, Gregory Akenzua (Enogie of Evbobanosa & Abudu)
- H.R.H, F.O. Iduozee (Enogie Evboesi)
- H.R.H P.O.Akenzua (Enogie of Orogho)
- H.R.H, O. Akenzua (Enogie of Oko-Odighi)
- H.R.H, Edun Akunzua (Enogie of Obazuwa)
- H.R.H, M. A. Ogiieriakhi (Enogie of Uvbe-Nisi)
- H.R.H, O.E.Obanosa (Enogie of Evbolekpen)
- H.R.H, A. Ogiemwonyi (Enogie of Utok)
- H.R.H, K.O. Omorose (Enogie of Ohoghobi)
- H.R.H, Edomwonyi O. Ogiegbaen (Enogie of Egbaen)
- H.R.H, K. Ogiesoba (Enogie of Oka-Umuoguohen)
- H.R.H, Osaro. Omoregie (Enogie of Uselu N' Ahor)
- H.R.H, Emwinmadomwan (Enogie of Amagba- Akengbuda)
- H.R.H, L I. Obarogie (Enogie of Umelu)
- H.R.H, Edugie O. Ogiugo (Enogie of Ugo-Niyekorhiomwon)
- H.R.H, E.A. Ediae (Enogie of Evbovbiuke)
- H.R.H, I. Oyemwense (Enogie of Ohovbe)
- H.R.H, H. A. Osawaru (Enogie of Ohovbe)
- H.R.H, Eki.I yawe (Enogie of Obazagbon)
- H.R.H, Idu Akenzua (Enogie of Oghobaghase)
- H.R.H, G. O. Aigbe (Enogie of Ukhiri-Osemwende)
- H.R.H, G. E Eweka (Enogie of Aideyanoba)
- H.R.H, Uwafiokun_Eweka (Enogie of Obagie -Uwafiokun)
- H.R.H, U Ivbievbokun (Enogie of Evbomodu)
- H.R.H, Osayenmwenre Osagie (Enogie of Umegbe)
- H.R.H, J. I Ewansiha (Enogie of Oheze)
- H.R.H, M. Ogbonmwan (Enogie of Ogheghe Osemwende)
- H.R.H, Ibie O. Okhionkpamwonyi (Enogie of Iguogbe)

- His Royal Highness, Felix E. Ọmọrọdiọn (Enogie of Evbohuan)

His Royal Highness Enogie Felix Omorodion of Evbohuan

- H.R.H, O. Aghaghowen (Enogie of Ogu)
- H.R.H, I. Ogbemudia (Enogie of Okhuokhuo)
- H.R.H, A. A.Eguavoen (Enogie of Idumwungha)
- H.R.H, O. Osemwengie (Enogie of Orior-Ozolua)
- H.R.H, C. E Eresoyen (Enogie of Irua-N' Owina)
- H.R.H, I. Agidigbi (Enogie of Utese)
- H.R.H, Aimuanmwosa (Enogie of Ilobi)
- H.R.H, R. O. Ogunbor (Enogie of Ukhiri-Eresoyen)
- H.R.H, D. O. Ogiomade (Enogie of Ugboko)
- H.R.H, Felix I. Ogiugo (Enogie of Ugo N' Iyekikpoba)
- H.R.H, Iyayomwangbe (Enogie of Umoghunmwon Zuagbor)
- H.R.H, Aiwerioghene. O. Iduriase (Enogie of Eyaen)
- H.R.H, Okunbor (Enogie of Evbomodu)
- H.R.H, A. Osagie (Enogie of Oye-Iyanomo)
- H.R.H, E. Osamogie (Enogie of Avbiama)
- H.R.H, E. Edomwonyi (Enogie of Ika)
- H.R.H, S.E. Aduwa Ogiegbaen (Enogie of Eyae)
- H.R.H, C. Ogieriakhi (Enogie of Uroho)
- H.R.H, E. Eresoyen (Enogie of Uhogue)
- H.R.H, A. Obanosa (Enogie of Iyekeze)
- H.R.H, L. Ugbo (Enogie of Ugha)
- H.R.H, O.Imadonmwinyi (Enogie of Obagie N'Evbosa)
- H.R.H, S. Ohangbon (Enogie of Evbomomo)
- H.R.H, E. Osarobo (Enogie of Idogbo)
- H.R.H, J.O. Igbinoghene (Enogie of Uholor)
- H.R.H, S.Omoragbon (Enogie of Idunmnungbo)
- H.R.H, Ogieayevbona Ivbaeniko (Enogie of Ukpera)
- H.R.H, C. Edomwonyi (Enogie of Erua)
- H.R.H, E. E. Owie (Enogie of Evbowe)
- H.R.H, Owie (Enogie of Evboerhen)
- H.R.H, E. D.I. Irobun (Enogie of Iguemokhua)
- H.R.H, I.O. Uwaifo (Enogie of Omolua Igbanke)
- H.R.H, O Igbinenikao (Enogie of Ute-Ekoko)
- H.R.H, O. Aghahowa (Enogie of Oghede)

- H.R.H, J.A. I.Ekhosu (Enogie of Oka N' Izevbihen)
- H.R.H, J.A. Edosomwan (Enogie of Azagba Okha)
- H.R.H, O. Onaghise (Enogie of Evboewedo)
- H.R.H, E. I. Omobuogie (Enogie of Ebazogie N'Ugo)
- H.R.H, I. Eguaevoen (Enogie of Orovie)
- H.R.H, I. Gbagbon (Enogie of Ahor)
- H.R.H, O.O. Eweka (Enogie of Use)
- H.R.H, O. Aiguobasiminogie (Enogie of Siluko)
- H.R.H, P.O. Uzamere (Enogie of Egba)
- H.R.H, E. Oyevbimina (Enogie of Owe)
- H.R.H, K.N. Udobor (Enogie of Ugolo)
- H.R.H, J.A. Airehenbuwa (Enogie of Obadan)
- H.R.H, Jeremiah Omorodion (Enogie of Igbontor Idumuiru Igbanke)
- H.R.H, Ikuobasoyemwen (Enogie of Igbekhue)
- H.R.H, S.E. Omoregie (Enogie of Ulegun)
- H.R.H, O. Idemudia (Enogie of Ewan)
- H.R.H, U.Iyengumwena (Enogie of Ume)
- H.R.H, Ewemade Uyimwengbaifo (Enogie of Ekae)
- H.R.H, D.O. Evbuomwan (Enogie of Umokpe Irua)
- H.R.H, I. Eresoyen (Enogie of Ogheghe)
- H.R.H, I. Idugboe (Enogie of Uwan-Esigie)
- H.R.H, Eghosa Agho (Enogie of Arah)
- H.R.H, O.A.A.U. Eweka (Enogie of Obagie)
- H.R.H, E. Obanosa (Enogie of Egbeaen)
- H.R.H, J. Ovonramwen (Enogie of Uwan-Eweka)

Enogie of Egbaen

(H.R.H Edomwonyi O. Ogiegbaen)

Enogie of Evbobanosa & Abudu

(H.R.H Gregory Akenzua)

Enogie of Eyaen

(H.R.H Aiwerioghene. O. Iduriase)

Enogie of Ebazogie N'Ugo

(H.R.H.E. I. Omobuogie)

Enogie of Ọbazuwa

(H.R.H Edun Akunzua)

Enogie of Iyekẹzẹ

(H.R.H A. Ọbanosa)

Enogie of Use

H.R.H O.O. Eweka

Enogie of Ọbagie

H.R.H O.A.A.U. Eweka

EKHAẸMWẸN (CHIEFS)

- Iyase of Benin (Chief S.U. Igbe)
- The Esama of Benin (Chief Igbinediọn)
- The Eriyo of Benin (Chief B.O. Okoro)
- Ero of Benin. Uzama Nihinron (Chief Ero)
- Ọyemwensoba of Benin (Chief D.O. Ebenghe)
- Ọbaguah Idase of Benin (Chief Joseph Ogieva)
- Banawo of Benin (Chief E.O.W. Banawo)
- Ekhoerosioba of Benin (Chief E.E. Igbinoba)
- Efeọbasota of Benin (Chief P.E. Okooboli)
- Obhon Uware of Benin (Chief U. Ọviasogie)
- Ọbazuwa of Benin (Chief O.U. Isekhure)
- Ezọmo of Benin (Chief Ezọmo)
- Ogiesughe of Benin (Chief Enoma Ogiesughe)
- Ezele of Benin (Chief O.U. Isekhurẹ)
- Chief O. Ekhatọr (Obobaifo of Benin)
- Aighọbahi of Benin (Chief O. Ọbasẹki)
- Esogban of Benin (Chief D.U. Edebiri)
- Aighọbahi of Benin (Chief O. Ọmoruyi)
- Usoh of Benin (Chief O. Eharevbai)
- Okawagha of Benin (Chief O. Na'Vbiogbe)
- Ọbamarhiaye of Benin (Chief Onghino)
- Osunma of Benin (Chief M.N. Ozibo Esere)
- Ede Ọba of Benin (Chief I. Idahosa)
- Ailefọba of Benin (Chief E. Idada)
- Aighọbahi of Benin (Chief J. Oko-Ogua)
- Osajiọbase of Benin (Chief P. Aigbogun)
- Isekhurẹ and the Chief priest of Benin (Chief Nosakhare Isekhurẹ)
- Ikpọnmwọnba of Benin (Chief T.N. Ọmọregie)
- Ọbadiaru of Benin (Chief N. Ọbadiaru)
- Agbọnmọba of Benin (Chief S.O.O Igiebọr)
- Akẹnuwa of Benin (Chief Oboh Osazuwa)
- Uwangue of Benin (Chief G. O. Aiweriọba

- Uwayọba of Benin (Chief S. Ogbẹwe)
- Uwayọba of Benin (Chief John. Igiehọn)
- Ọvienmọba of Benin (Chief O. Udubọr)
- Aigbọvọba of Benin (Chief O. Ọhẹnhẹn)
- Esere Of Benin (Chief S.O. Ọbamwọnyi)
- Ọlaye of Benin (Chief Abeliehigie)
- Aigbọvọba of Benin (Chief A. Aigbogun)
- Osaguẹ of Benin (Chief D.O. Idabie)
- Ọbaradesuwa of Benin (Chief D.E Osifo)
- Ine Of Benin (Chief E. U. Uzamere)
- Aiyọbahan of Benin (Chief O. Adun)
- Oweto of Benin (Chief I. Airihenbuwa)
- Akẹnuwa of Benin (Chief J.O. Osazuwa)
- Osasuoba of Benin (Chief S.O. Ọmọrogbe)
- Oliha of Benin (Chief Ediọnwe Oliha)
- Ọbarisiagbon of Benin (Chief S.O. Ọmọrogbẹ
- Ọbazuaye of Benin (Chief Edọmwandagbọn)
- Aitenghoba of Benin (Chief J.O. Osazuwa)
- Ọbazelu of Benin (Chief Osaro Idah)
- Ologboshẹrẹ of Benin (Chief O. O. Ologboshere)
- Obo-Ọbairuwa of Benin (Chief N. Uwadia)
- Ọkayobọghae of Benin (Chief J.O Ajay)
- Ọbaradesagbọn of Benin (Chief iguobarueghian)
- Ogiefa Nọrmuekpo of Benin (Chief Amadin Ogiefa)
- Oshodin Of Benin (Chief Dan Iyamu)
- Ọbasogie of Benin (Chief E. A. Obasogie)
- Ogiefa Nọrmuekpo of Benin (Chief Amadin Ogiefa)
- The Eriere Of Benin (Chief Ọviasogie)
- The Oloton of Benin (Chief Oloton)
- Ogiefa of Benin (Chief Agonhikpakpa Ogiefa)
- The Ekhoẹgua Benin (Chief M.E. Nehizena)
- Osaivbie of Benin (Chief O. S. Ogbẹide)

Sir (Dr) Chief Gabriel Osawaru Igbinediọn

LLD, D. LITT, GCK. The Esama of Benin Kingdom

Chief S.U. Igbẹ

(The Iyasẹ of Benin kingdom)

LIST OF ESANLAND ENIJIE

- HRH, E. Izebhiokhai I (Onojie of Okalo and the Enobagie of Esanland)
- HEH, W.E. Ighodalo II (Onojie of Ujiogba)
- HRH, Zaiki (barr.) Anthony Ehizojie Abumere II (Enojie of Ekpoma)
- HRH. Solomon Ojeaga Izuware I (Onojie of Ujiogba)
- HEH, E. Eluojierior I (JP) (Onojie of Igueben and Okaigun of Esanland)
- HRH, W.O. Momodu II (JP) (Ojirrua of Irrua and Okaijesan of Esanland)
- HEH, Oboh Ehizogie I (Onojie of Ugun)
- HRH, J. E. Ukato (JP) (Onojie of Ugboha)
- HRH, S.I. Obade II (JP) (Onogie of Ugbegub)
- HRH, Emos Akhadia (Onojie of Amahor)
- HRH, O. G. Abumere (Onojie of Ubiaja)
- HRH, B. A. Iluobe (Regent of Uzea)
- HRH, S. O. Aidenogie I (Onojie of Ewossa)
- HRH, D. B. Offor (Clan head of Urhu)
- HRH. Anselm Aidenojie (Onojie of Uromi)
- HRH, Ogbidi Okojie (Onojie of Uromi) (1857 – February 3, 1944)
- HRH, Otoikhine 1, Uwuigbowen Otaokhine Dominic (Onojie of Urohi)
- HRH Stephen Ukato (Onojie of Ugboha)

Enogie of Ewohimi January 27, 1959

HRH. Anselm Aidenojie

The Onojie of Uromi

HRH L Peter Usifoh Ojiefoh (ii)

The Onojie of Ewohimi

HRH Uwuigbowen Otaokhine Dominic

The Onojie of Urohi

ESAN CLANS

AMAHOR
EBELLE
EGORO New
EKPON
EKPOMA New
EMU
EWATTO
EWOHIMI
EWU
IDOA
IFEKU
IGUEBEN
ILLUSHI
IRRUA
IYENLEN
KEKHENLEN
OGWA
OHORDUA
OKALO
OkHUESAN
OPOJI
ORIA
OROWA
UGBEGUN
UBIAJA
UDO
UGBOHA
UGUN
UJIOGBA
UKHUN
URHOHI
UROMI
UROHI
UZEA
WOSSA

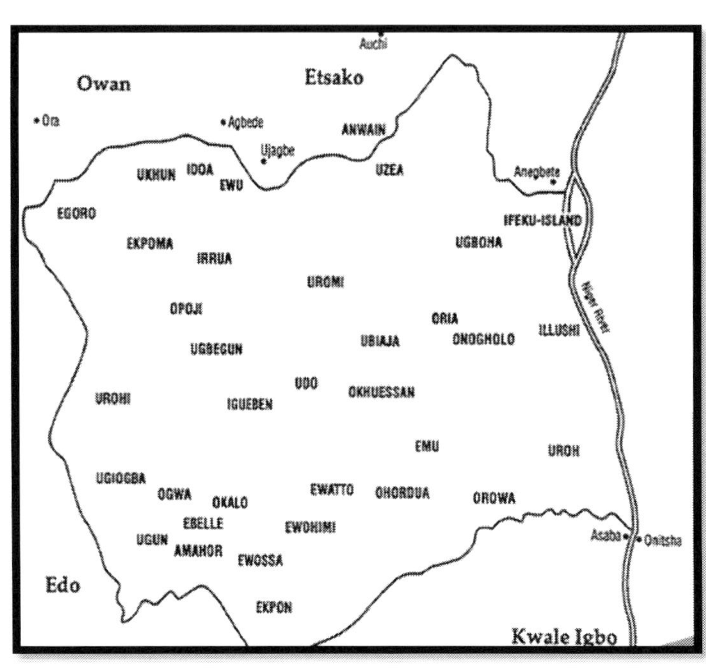

Reverend Dr. Chris Oyakhilome

SOME COMMOM WORDS IN ESAN

Baby	/	Ọmọn	You	/	uwẹ
Babies	/	Imọn	He	/	Ole
Male	/	Ọmọle	She	/	Olle
Man	/	Okpea	We	/	Iman
Men	/	Ikpea	They	/	Ele
Woman	/	Okhuo	Beautiful	/	Bhon ose
Women	/	Ikhuo	Deaf	/	Yi eho
Relation	/	Obhio	Blind	/	Rui ẹlo
Relations	/	Ibhio	Sweet	/	Mhẹn bli unu
Child	/	Obhokhan	Fish	/	Ehenlen
Children	/	Ibhokhan	Elephant	/	Eni
Boy	/Usẹnbhokhan		Disgrace	/	Efa
Girl	/	Ọmọhin	Eyes	/	Elolo
Elder	/	Ọwanlẹn	Pepper	/	Esin
Person	/	Ọrhia	Finish	/	Fo
Stone	/	Udo	Serve	/	Ga
School	/	Uwaebe	Cover	/	Gue
Stick	/	Eran	Lay	/	Ho
Something	/	Emhin	Regret	/	He
Money	/	Igho	Climb	/	Henlen
Feathers	/	Igen	Wash	/	Hoo
Grave	/	Idin	Market	/	Ẹki
Laugh	/	Jie	Chair	/	Aga
Send	/	jie	Dog	/	Awa

ESAN NUMERALS

Okpa / One

Eva / Two

Ea / Three

Enẹn / Four

Isẹn / Five

Ehan / Six

Ihinlọn / Seven

Elẹnlẹn / Eight

Isinlin / Nine

Igbe / Ten

Ugie / Twenty

Ọgban / Thirty

Egbolo Eva / Fourty

Igbe-yan-Egboeva/ Fifty

Iyeha / Sixty

Igbe-yan-Iyeha/ Seventy

Iyenẹn / Eighty

Igbe-yan-Iyenen/ Ninety

Iyesen / Hundred

Iyeisen-Eva / Two Hundred

Iyisẹn Ea / Three Hundred

Iyisẹn-Enen / Four Hundred

Iyisẹn- Isen / Five Hundred

Iyisen-Igbe (Uli)/ One Thousand

Ebo / One Million

Spice Vision
Musician (Ọkpemaba)
Ovbi' Ẹdo

Hon. Newman Ugiagbe
Politician, Entrepreneur, Philanthropist

Ifasẹ Davies (Benin Girl)

SOME ẸDO MUSICIANS AND ACTORS

MUSICIANS (AVB'KPEMA)

The Talent of Benin

Chris ID

Isaac Black (Ọmọ Nọzozo)

Sir Patrick Idahosa

Uncle Zack

Felix Liberty

Sir Victor Uwaifo

Chief L Osula

Agbakpan Olita

Dombrayẹ Aghama

Alaska Agho

Fabomo

Ivbiye dance band

Uselu motor park

Uyi Talent

Wonderful twin

Olẹtin Superstar

Collins Ọkẹ

Bengi Igbahumhe

Constance Bolivia

Olita

Adviser Nowamagbe

Idada (Don Dada)

Uyi Cole

Osahẹnọma Esewi

Princess Marian light Alilẹ

Prince Artor Segun Alilẹ

Idemudia Cole

Da Silva (Ẹghosa Osawaru

Xaint Destiny

Ukodo

Wonderful twins

Adazẹ

Mochico bay

IK Noble

Oriri

Adamosa

Maleke Idowu

Amin man

Esther Ẹdọkpayi lady

Lobito Aghaowa

Rema

Osarọ Nomayo

Chief J O Ọmọruyi

Stanley O Iyọnawan

Ọmọregie Eguasa

Ọhẹnhẹn

The Talented Star

Prince Clement Ogie

Samson Aigbọbo

C E Umumarogie

Don Cliff toosmile

Robinson

Bayo Ade

Easy Quest

Mongo park

Black IQ

Counsellor O Idehẹn

Palmer Ọmọruyi

Apostle Ọgbọmwan

Sister Naomi

China White

Ehritiho Solẹsolẹ

Slizzy E

Spice Vision

Manfesto

Monday Dollar Ojo

Jacky Sula

AG Simili

24Bits

Vivy Melody

Okpẹranky Aziegbemwin

Sir Pauligo

King Famous Esere

J froze

Don VS

Influence Akaba

Jetplay

DJ Choplife (UK)

TTY (Italy)

Beckleys Ọkẹ

Lady Erosion

Kizo Odaro

Benin Girl (Davies Ifasẹ)

Oligbese

Sir Victor Uwaifo | AkabaMan | Osayọmọre Joseph

Wilson Ẹhigiatọr | Majek Fashek | Emperor Wadada Aikore

ACTORS/ACTRESSES

Ọmọbalance

Kenedy Uyi Ọviahọn

Amẹnaghawọn Imasuẹn

IK Kevin

Silvester Uwadiae.

Sharon Okpamẹn.

Degbueyi Ọviahọn.

Greg Igbinosun.

Sandra Aigbogun.

Jolly Noga.

Friday Enọgheghase.

Aisọsa Evbenaye.

Precious Osayande.

Osasuyi West

Ẹwẹka Osawemwenze

Lucky Ọmọigui

Esther Edọkpayi

Jerry Angel

Queen Alubogie

Ifaluyi (Richie)

Pat Usoh

Ẹbony Ọbasuyi

Prince Eni Ọbasuyi

Austin Nyz Ovbiebo

Johnbull Eghianruwa

Shine Ọsẹmwinigie

Alex Nosa

Eunice Ọmọregie

Mercy Aigbe

Nosa Ọbaseki

Nosa rex

Jemima Osunde

Adesua Etomi

Favour Ọriakhi

Francess Okungbowa

Juliet Esey Joseph

Ik Osakioduwa

Vahilio Osagie

Prince Olotu

Best Ogunmu

Patience I Ọmọruyi

Billy kings

Ẹhigiatọr Nosa Joy

Florence Iyamu

Young Elder

Mcee Twinko

Ehi Buckler Isibọr

Nosa Ọbasẹki

Loveth Azugbene

Moses Ọbakpọlọr

SOME FACES AND NAMES OF ẸDO SONS AND DAUGHTERS

Dillon Sandoka Uwa Ọviahọn Princess Chi. Ivie

M Urhoghide Dennis Idahosa J I Idehen Osa Ọmọregie

Honourable Osarọ Ọbazẹ Professor Ambrose Folorunsho Alli

(Former Oredo Local Gov. Chairman)(Former Exe. Governor of Bendel State)

Meredith

Osagie O

Sharon

Kevin

Nosa Rex

Kazeem

Dr. E Ighodaro

Priest H Imafu

Chief Ọmẹdẹ Isi Edrick Justus

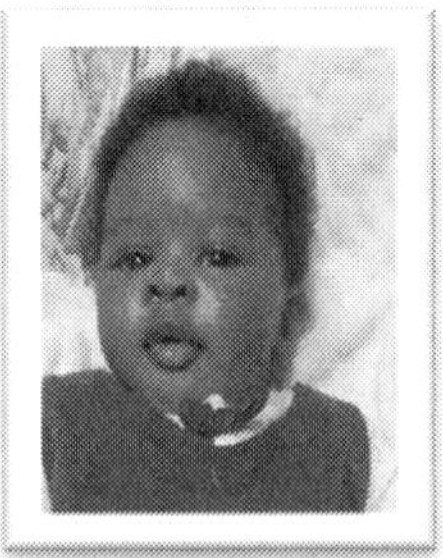

Ọmọsukpọn

Sheikh Don Jeff

Marris Iyamu

Uwaila

TTY

Ẹfe Bluejeans

Charles O

Charles Ighodaro

Efenọsun

(Businessman)

Eghosa

(Entrepreneur)

Eghafona

(Pastor)

R Igharo

(Prison officer UK)

Archbishop Benson Idahosa (A Charismatic preacher and founder of Church of God Mission International)

Archbishop John Edokpọlọr

Bright Enọbakhare

Monday Dollar Ojo

Chief Anthony Anenih

Chief Francis Ẹdo-Osagie

Chief Jacob U. Egharevba

Chief Anthony Enahọrọ

Dr. Pius Egberanmwen Odubu (formal Deputy Governor of Ẹdo State)

Demi Isaac Ọviawe

Vivy Melody

Dr Abel Guọbadia

Eghosa Asẹmota Agbonifo

Felix Idubọr

Felix Liberty

Godwin Osagie Abbe

Professor Osasẹre Orumwense,

Ẹhizigie Ogbẹbọr (CEO of Sayaveth Interiors and Hotel and Philanthropist)

Professor Osayuki Godwin Oshodin

Hakeem Belo-Osagie (Entrepreneur and philanthropist)

Pastor Chris Oyakhilome

Professor Festus Iyayi

Suyi Davies Okungbọwa

Samuel Ogbemudia

John Ọdigie Oyegun

Captain Idahosa (Hosa) Wells Okunbọ

Business magnate, investor, philanthropist and trained commercial pilot

The Imafidons

The Smartest family in Britain

Sir Ọmọruyi Olotun

CEO Uyi Technical/ Uyi Grand Hotel

Apostle S.E. Ọgbọmwan

Founder C.A.C.G.M International

Julian Osula

Business magnate and investor

Daisy Ehanire Danjuma

Politician and a Businesswoman

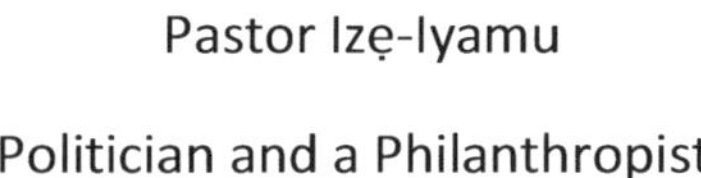

Pastor Izẹ-Iyamu

Politician and a Philanthropist

Chief Amb. Osarọdiọn Osagie

President A Godsent Foundation

Prof. Martins Agbọnlahọr

Journalist, Columnist and Author.

Ibosa Oshodin is an Ẹdo
Philanthropist and property investor

Ọmọsẹde Gabriella Igbinediọn
Barrister, Politician and Philanthropist

Rosenary Osula

CEO Rosula Foundation

Westley Asoro

Politician and CEO Westley Hotels

Hon. Matthew Iduoriyekemwẹn

Politician, Businessman and Philanthropist.

Charles Inojie

Actor, Comedian and Movie Producer

Charles O

Linda Osifo

Slizzy E

Sandra

Lancelot Oduwa Imasuẹn

Legendary Film Director and Producer (D'Guv and the Boss)

Amẹn Imasuẹn

Film director/ Producer

Amẹn Imasuẹn was born into the family of chief and Mrs Godwin Imasuen in Benin City, Ẹdo state. Amẹn attended Ugbọwọ primary school, Adọlọr collage, both In Benin City, later advanced to the prestigious Auchi Polytechnic in Ẹdo State, where he studied Mass Communication. He began his early career as a Production Assistant under Ambassador Lancelot Oduwa Imasuen (The Boss and award-winning film director/producer) where he was trained as a filmmaker, he made his first movie at the age of 22 years (Ewọwọ), an Ẹdo language movie blockbuster that earned him a lot of attention. Amẹn Imasuẹn has since directed over 30 movies.

Dr Samuel Ogbẹmudia
Formal Exe. Governor of Bendel State

Engr. Abel Osaigbọvo
Chemical Engineer

Richie John Ọnaiwu

Businessman, Investor, Philanthropist and Entertainer

Richie John Ọnaiwu is President of RichieRich Global Limited, an organisation that specialises in Real Estate with development Portfolios across multiple countries. Mr Ọnaiwu is an eminent cultural and social entrepreneur who is also CEO and Founder of RichieRich Entertainment a successful United Kingdom based events company.

Blessing Agho

Founder, EarthTab Farm Hub

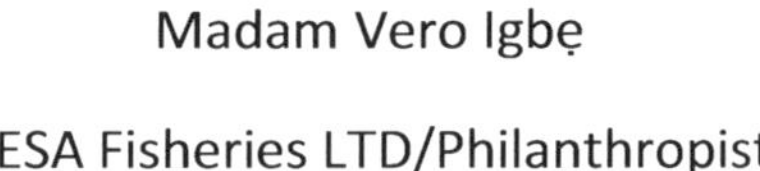

Madam Vero Igbẹ

VESA Fisheries LTD/Philanthropist

Loretta Oduware Oghoro-Okor

Health Care Practitioner (Doctor), Entrepreneur, Motivational Speaker, Writer, Mentor, Humanitarian, Author, Health Advocate, Educationist, Blogger, Activist, Researcher, Entertainer and Philanthropist.

Mr Lucky Oseye

CEO and Founder, AFRO CODE and Global Interest ONLUS

Ẹki

Don VS

DJ Budetee

Julie Dala

Beatrice Ọmẹdẹ

EasyQuest

Adesua

Mr & Mrs Enaruna

Destiny Ebagua

George Ọnaifo

Kate Victor

Victor James

Black George

Albert Ọbazẹ

Pastor Okosun

Ẹdowaye O

Eunice Ọmọruyi

SA Patricia I Amadin

Ebony Ọbasuyi

Dqueen Adesuwa

MC Ẹdo Pikin

Princess Doris O Ọ

Lady Joy

ỌmọBalance

Esther Ẹdọkpayi

Ik Osakioduwa

Mercy Aigbe

Rema

Jennifer Ọbasẹki

Joy Ọbazẹ

Osagie Ẹlẹgbẹ

Mc Jerry Angel

Osaretin Daniel Igbinosa (AKA Robonto)

Entrepreneur, Medical Assistant, Entertainer, interior designer, Humanitarian and Philanthropist (CEO Sodi interior Decor and Contractor)

Uselu Humanitarian Development Initiative (NGO)

AKA Uselu to the World

Hon. Evans Agbọnwanegbe (Current Chairman, UHDI)

Uselu to the World (N' Ẹdo ghama) is a group of male and female who grew up in Uselu and Environs in Edo State, Nigeria coming together for harmony and to help Eradicate Female Genital Mutilation, Human Trafficking and helping those living in the street.

<u>Graciousgift Usuno Aka-Ukinebo</u>
Entrepreneur, Investor, Motivational Speaker, Humanitarian, Healthcare Practitioner, Philanthropist and Promotes Healthy lifestyle/ wellbeing.

SOME ẸDO SONS AND DAUGHTERS IN VARIOUS SPORTS GLOBALLY

Daisy Osakue / Italian National Champion-Discus Throw

Sunday Oliseh / Footballer (Born in Abavo, Delta State)

Gabriel Agbonlahor / (Aston Villa) The most honest footballer in history

Yukubu Ayebeni / Footballer (Born in Benin City)

Victor Mosse / Footballer

Wilfred Agbonivbare / Footballer

Jayson O Ọbazuaye / Basketball

Augustine Eguavoen / Footballer

Ọdion Jude Ighalo / Footballer

Andre Iguadala / Basketball

Julius Aghahuwa / Footballer

Drew Uyi / Fa Licensed Football Agent, management, and media

Austin Eguaevoen / Footballer

Wilson Oruma / Footballer

Friday Elahọr / Footballer

Peter Osazẹ Ọdewingie / Footballer

Thompson Oliha / Footballer

Sergio Osahọn Uyi / Footballer

Bright Ọmọkaro / Footballer

Kevin Ọmẹdẹ / Football/Sprinting

David Oseye	/	Footballer/Model
Thomsom Oliha	/	Footballer
Julius Aghahowa	/	Footballer
Kamarudeen Usman	/	UFC
Christopher Ogie	/	Basketball (Ridgebacks)
Arene Iyekekpọlọr	/	Basketball
Matthew Osunde	/	Basketball
Giulio Osariemẹn	/	Footballer

Ọdiọn Jude Ighalo

Ọdiọn Jude Ighalo is a Nigerian footballer from Edo State, who plays for the English Premier League (EPL) side, Manchester United. Ighalo is a top Nigerian legend who is one of the greatest and most famous footballers the nation has ever produced in the history of international football.

Daisy Osakue

Julius Aghahuwa

Sidney Ewẹka

Osazẹ Ọdewingie

Kamarudeen Usman

Drew Uyi

ẸDO NATIONAL ANTHEM

Ọba Ẹware mwẹn n'ogie n'igho

Ovbiẹ Ẹkẹnẹkẹnẹ ma dẹyọọ

Ugha de vbẹ umuọdia

Ana ren ruen oh

Tugha tọ gbe'gie re

Ọba gha tọkpẹre

Isẹ ise

Ọba gha tọkpẹre

Isẹ ise

Enikaro ọyawewẹ Ọba mwan oh

E tugha tọ gbe'gie re

Enikaro ọyawewẹ Ọba mwan oh

E tugha tọ gbe'gie re

ẸDO CREST

ẸDO MAP

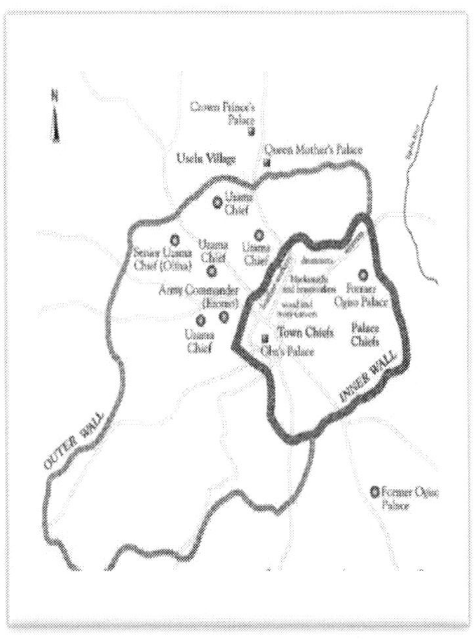
N
Crown Prince's Palace
Queen Mother's Palace
Uselu Village
Uzama Chief
Senior Uzama Chief (Oliha)
Uzama Chief
Uzama Chief
Army Commander (Ezomo)
Former Ogiso Palace
Town Chiefs
Palace Chiefs
Uzama Chief
Oba's Palace
INNER WALL
OUTER WALL
Former Ogiso Palace

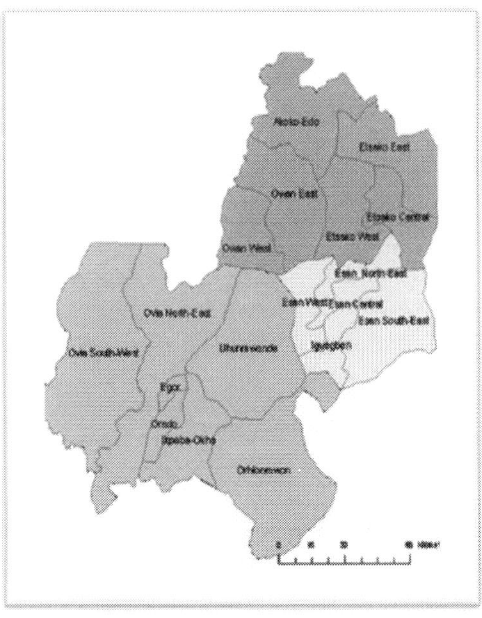
Akoko-Edo
Etsako East
Owan East
Etsako Central
Etsako West
Owan West
Esan North-East
Ovia North-East
Esan West
Esan Central
Esan South-East
Ovia South-West
Uhunmwonde
Igueben
Egor
Oredo
Ikpoba-Okha
Orhionmwon

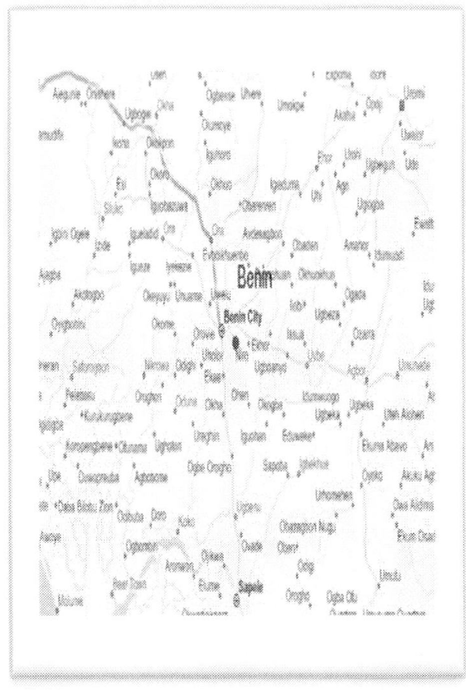
Benin
Benin City
Sapele

SOME ẸDO ARTIFACTS AND THE BENIN MOAT

Ada **Ẹgogo (Bell)** **Ẹbẹn**

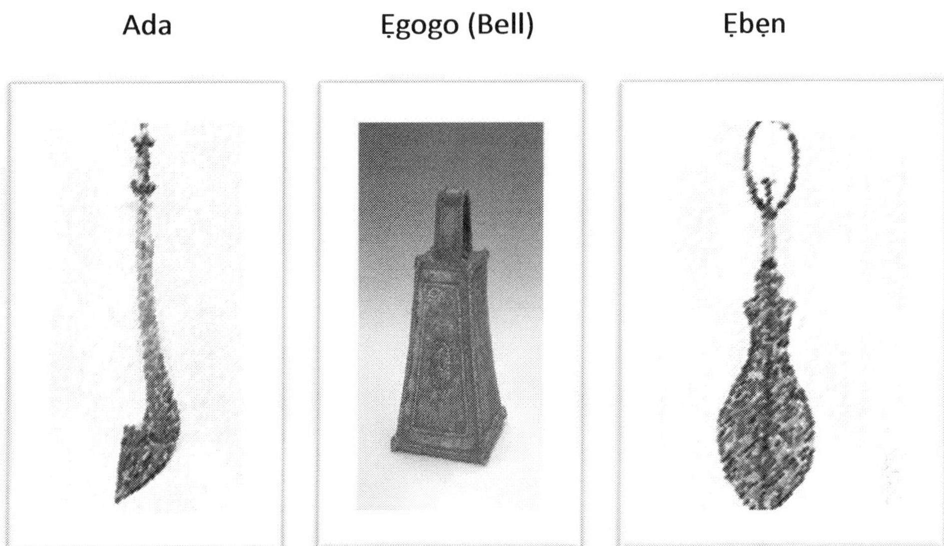

The Benin Moat (Iya)

The Benin moat, also known traditionally as Iya, is the largest man-made earthwork in the world.

Emotan

Idia nẹ Iyẹ Ẹsigie

Arhuan N' Okemezi (The Great)

The Duke of Udo

IGUN STREET – THE HOME OF BRONZE CASTING IN BENIN CITY

Source of photographs (Google images)

SOME MORE FACES AND NAMES OF ẸDO SONS AND DAUGHTERS

Ọmọrẹgbẹ Erediauwa

Adesua Etomi

Emotan Shine

Degbuẹyi Ọviahọn

Itohan P Ọmọregie

Sandra Idubọr

AG Silimi

Nẹkpẹn Ọbasuyi

PRAISES FOR THE GREAT OBA OF BENIN KINGDOM

Umogun Oza / The Child of the Oba whose mother hailed from Oza

Ekpẹn N' Owa / The home Tiger

Ovbi' Adimila / The son of Adimila

Ikeji Orisa / Second in command to the gods

Agbaghẹ N'Ovbi Olokun / Olokun's son, the cynosure of all mortals

Abieyuwa N'Ovbi Odua N'uhe / The son of the wealthy Odua of Uhe.

Ovbi' Ada, Ovbi' Ẹbẹn / The child of the owner of the Ada (Scimitar) and Eben (Royal Sword) Edo Symbol of Sovereignty.

Ovbi'Ekẹnẹkẹnẹ ma dẹyo / The son of beauty that never fades.

Ovbi'Ekuaho N'Olọ / The son of the rocky arm, the brave and powerful

Ovbie Ikpinhianbọ kpuru no Gb'oduma / The son of the short-fingered man that was still able to kill a lion

Nọhiẹn utete no gh'ughe s'ọmwan / The king on a hill, who sees more than everybody

Ovbi'Ọghonwan nei bun aro / The son of the fearless, who looks without twinkling his eyes

Ovbi'ode, ode n'ọhan ren mu' ete / The son of the warrior whose enemies got frightened at the announcement of the approach

Uku Akpọlọkpọlọ / The mighty that rules

Ovbi' Adọlọ nọ dọlo uwa dolo utọmwẹn / The son of the wise judge and peace maker who combined wisdom and wealth with long life

Ovbi' oven owie nọ gbaisi / The son of the morning sun that covers everywhere

Ovbi' Akpogunla, ogie no y'igho b'owa / The child of the womb of Akpogunla – the warrior who fought big wars and built a house of cowries

Ọba n'osa / A king that is god

Ovbi' otolo n'olomi; Ologberọnmwọn nei rie iruẹn, ebo, ayemwinre eminiminimini / The son of the water controller, the son

of beauty itself, the starter of things and the person whose reign saw people with many tongues.

ỌBA GHATỌ KPẸRẸ

ISẸ!!!

SOME MORE FACES AND NAMES OF ẸDO SONS AND DAUGHTERS

Hilary Ọsẹmwẹngie

Best Ogunmu

Skimmy Yah

Daniel Moses

Princess Peters

Oloye E. Oloye

Chief Efe Imaghodọ

Davido & Mum (Imade)

Joyce Ọbasẹki

Dr. (Mrs.) Zuwaire Doreen Yusuf

(Educationist and a Philanthropist)

Francis Agoda AKA I GO DYE

(Comedian and a Philanthropist)

Olumide Akpata

Legal Practitioner and a Philanthropist

Mc Allamano

(Comedian and a Philanthropist)

Becky Okhis (AKA: Lady B)

CEO: B & E Enterprises

Entrepreneur, Investor, Humanitarian and Philanthropist

Dr Ọsẹmwẹngie Osatohanmwẹn

Nigerian Born Engineer Dr Ọsẹmwẹngie Osatohanmwẹn has 4 PhDs and 7 Master's Degrees. He makes drones for the US Army.

"A people without the knowledge of their past history, origin and culture is like a tree without roots." Marcus Garvey.

Osazuwa Ọmẹdẹ Multimedia

NON FICTION

Osazuwa Ọmẹdẹ has produced a gripping narrative for his native Ẹdo indigenes – Martins Agbọnlahọr, Author of *Killing Them Softly*.

In this age of cultural awareness, it has become imperative to identify one's self with his culture as well as his spoken dialect. This is necessary especially in a volatile country like Nigeria where the majority ethnic groups are preponderant over their minority counterparts and in so doing, reducing these groups to mere irrelevance. The persuasive inference one can draw from this, therefore, is that if these ethnic languages are left unused or sparsely used, they will fizzle out in the near future – and we will be worse for it.

Waghiaghaz'Ẹdo in this respect, is a useful guide to learning the Ẹdo, one of the minority tribes in Nigeria. It introduces readers to its alphabets, consonants as well as its pronunciation. In fact, call it a succinct appraisal of the cultural as well as ancestral heritage of the Ẹdo people and you are not far from it.

Osazuwa Ọmẹdẹ has produced a captivating work for his ethnic Edo tribe so much so that when you flip its first pages, you are spellbound to read it through to the end.

Osazuwa Ọmẹdẹ is an historian, writer, photography enthusiast and a film producer based in the United Kingdom. He has deep interest in the preservation of the rich cultural heritage of his ancestral Ẹdo tribe and her people. He holds a B.Sc. (Hons) in Oil and Gas Management from Plymouth University.

Some of his creation include: Wrong Desire (a movie), Odumamwẹn (a movie) as well as a Book titled 'Business Privileges in Nigeria.'

Mr Ọmẹdẹ is the Founder/President of Osazuwa Ọmẹdẹ Multimedia based in the United Kingdom. He is also a co-creator of Africa Couples Connect and the Osazuwa Ọmẹdẹ Smile Project (an NGO). He is a reserved gentleman of ample knowledge.

Email: omedeosazuwa@hotmail.co.uk